D1074670

books by Ray Miller

The Ford Rd Series

The Chevy Chase Series

The AUTOBAHN Series

CAMARO!
Chevy's *Classy* Chassis

An Illustrated History

By RAY MILLER

The Evergreen Press
Avalon, California

CAMARO!
Chevy's *Classy* Chassis

First Printing
April 1981

Seventh Printing
November 1991

Library of Congress Catalog Card #80-70286
ISBN 0-913056-10-3

Copyright Ray Miller 1981

Printed by:
  Sierra Printers, Inc.
  Bakersfield, California

Typesetting by:
  Lockwood Litho
  Oceanside, California

Photo processing by:
  KJM Photo/Graphics
  Sebastopol, California

Printed in U.S.A.

The Evergreen Press
P.O. Box 306
Avalon, California 90704

RAY MILLER, an Oceanside, California resident for over ten years has devoted himself to providing an unusual series (actually *two* series) of books in which specific cars are covered in photographical detail never before attempted. Described variously as "an absolute must", "for fans who like to look at old Chevys", "Top quality photographic reporting", his books have received an acceptance unmatched by many.

Beginning in 1971 with the publication of FROM HERE TO OBSCURITY which he co-authored with Bruce McCalley, editor of *THE VINTAGE FORD*, his efforts picked up speed as he produced HENRY'S LADY and THE V-8 AFFAIR which dealt with the pre-war Fords. Then came THUNDER-BIRD!, followed shortly by The Real CORVETTE, NIFTY-FIFTIES Fords, and the two-volume in-depth study CHEVROLET: Coming of Age, and CHEVROLET: USA #1. MUSTANG Does It! was his most recent book, and this amply qualifies him to author this newest work, CAMARO! Chevy's *Classy* Chassis.

This book brings to four the number of volumes in the popular CHEVY CHASE SERIES (the Ford books are grouped as The FORD ROAD SERIES) and permits the reader the opportunity to note the similarities as well as the differences among the Chevrolet automobile lines.

RAY has been interested in cars for many years, having owned and driven both Ford and also Chevrolet products. With characteristic enthusiasm, his approach to these books encourages his purchase and restoration of subject vehicles, hence his collection has now grown to include not one, but *two* Camaros. In addition to owning the beautiful Pace Car convertible on the dust jacket of this book he also owns an excellent 1968 Z-28, "the hottest car I have ever driven", he reports.

Southern California is particularly well adapted to works of this type. With the excellent year-round weather, automobiles do not suffer the destruction by the elements to the degree that they do elsewhere. Thus, many fine cars remain in service for far longer periods and can be seen daily on the Freeways. From this source are selected those cars which are used for illustrative models. It is RAY MILLER's exceptional skill in making appropriate determinations that enable a reference book such as this to be prepared.

The Author wishes to thank those who contributed so much of their time and their interest towards making this a better book than it might otherwise have become.

The Owners, generally mentioned by name within the text of this book, are again thanked. Their patient understanding of the needs of the photographer and their willingness to share with him the nuances of their own special discoveries have advanced the cause. Their patience in allowing us to crawl over, under, and through, their beautiful automobiles has permitted us to present these unique views.

RON ZINDARS and JOHN ANDERSON of Z & Z Auto in Orange, California, posess a huge collection of Camaro parts and were not only gracious enough to educate us, but provided so many of these parts for detail pictures that we were truly amazed.

JIM ROHN, of Phoenix, and LARRY ZIEDMAN of Culver City, California, both "parts scroungers extraordinaire", were most cooperative in placing many of their rare parts before our cameras.

STAN CLAPPER, of Clinton, Wisconsin, located the magnificent Pace Car convertible on the dust jacket of this book and drove that car from Chicago to Los Angeles in support of his belief that "Camaro *is* Chevy's *classy* chassis".

MARK SMITH, of Specialized Investments of Houston, provided us not only with advice and information on the elusive Cross Ram manifold, but took the additional step of providing photographs of details that we had never before seen.

RALPH KRAMER and SUZANNE KANE of Chevrolet's Public Relations Office were most enthusiastic and encouraging. Their interest in the project resulted in an extraordinary amount of detail information that might otherwise have been overlooked.

The contribution of JERRY BECKER of Chevy Parts Ltd. in El Cajon, California cannot be too heavily applauded. Despite his busy schedule, Jerry accepted innumerable telephone calls from the Author seeking to verify a part or an application. Jerry's large stock of parts was opened to our camara as well and resulted in many of the accompanying illustrations.

Our friend GREG MULLENDORE of San Diego, a dedicated Camaro enthusiast, deserves a very special thanks, for Greg, whose job places him almost constantly on the California freeways, brought to our attention many of the photogenic cars shown here. By hailing the owners and identifying them for us, he succeeded in making our job far easier.

To all of these, and to the far greater number whose names may *not* appear in these pages, we again express our gratitude for their interest, their help, and their encouragement. This book is a better effort for their help.

rjm

In the Fall of 1966, some two and a half years after its major competitor had shown the way, giant General Motors Corporation brought to the marketplace a new car designed to staunch the flow of buyers flocking to Ford's new Mustang. Based largely on the characteristics of that competing car, the dimensions of the new GM products were almost identical, the styling extremely similar, and the price highly competitive.

By the time that Chevrolet's new Camaro appeared, Ford had already sold over one *million* of their new Mustangs, creating both a demand from new customers and also a market within for the now-loyal owners. It had been incumbent upon GM to respond, and their response was an extremely effective one.

First revealed to the public on September 12, 1966, its body shell would remain fundamentally unchanged for three model years, and then, after its first substantial change, continue almost unaltered for another twelve! Throughout these 15 years, the car retained its own special characteristics, performance, handling ease, comfort, and distinctive appearance. At first a somewhat undersized car, it appeared even smaller as conventional cars grew in the early '70's, but by 1980, when the others had been down-sized it appeared almost ponderous.

Camaro *was* a sporty car; it went with ease to the fun places of the era. Driving an early convertible Camaro with the top down was an enjoyment long remembered. It offered a quiet, almost docile, trip to the Supermarket, but at the same time, some production versions of the car came off of the showroom floor ready to compete as racing vehicles. With special preparations, including stuffing over-size power plants into its commodious engine compartment, it performed outstandingly on the race circuit.

Thus was, and is, the *classy* Chevrolet. Other models are larger, some more powerful, some more aggressive, and some more solid, but the Camaro offers response, comfort, distinctive appearance, and most of all, total enjoyment.

Come with us now and follow the changes in an unchanging car, CAMARO!, Chevy's *classy* Chassis . . .

"Let's face it," says a Chevy spokesman, "the other fellow showed everybody that the market exists for this type of car."

SPORTS ILLUSTRATED
September 19, 1966

By the Fall of 1966, Chevrolet had caught up; their newly-introduced Camaro looked like a winner. Its style was entirely new to Chevrolet; longer hood, shorter rear deck, low price, lean look, and loaded with optional equipment.

It was all of these, but one thing that it was not was original. The car that it was designed to resemble had been on the market for almost two and a half years, had sold well over one million, and was a competitor's product.

It takes a lot publicly to admit having been scooped by the competition; it simply is unpleasant so to do. Certainly Chevrolet never rushed to advertise a comparison with the competing product.

Only one unknown "Chevy Spokesman" voiced the thought however that had to be on everyone's mind. To him, for his willingness to speak the obvious, his candor, and his accuracy, we happily dedicate this book.

In presenting his material, the Author has made no attempt to isolate the cars except by model year. Since we have been attempting to describe the *characteristics* of a given year, we have deliberately employed those pictures which best served the immediate purpose. *For this reason, adjacent photos may not necessarily show views of the same car!*

We have attempted to screen the inaccuracies; we trust that we may have succeeded in this effort. This book was intended to be what it is, a compendium of information that will enable an observer to identify and to classify both cars and also parts. If there are errors, they are neither to our knowledge nor are they intentional.

TABLE OF CONTENTS

FRONT END RECOGNITION

1967 Standard

1967 RS

1968 Standard

1967 SS

1968 RS

1968 SS

1969 RS

1969 Standard

1969 SS

1970 Standard

1970 RS

1971 Standard

1972 Standard

13

1973 Rally Sport

1973 Type LT grill

1974

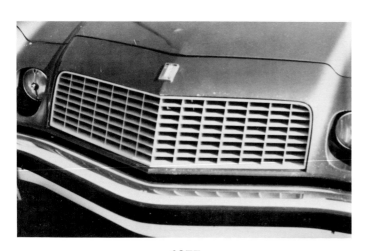

1975

1976

1977

1978 Type LT

1979 Z28

1979 Rally Sport

1980-81

1981 Z28

Dupin (1817) in which a ridiculous character, a draper, is called M. Calicot.)

calot, *sb.m.* 1. Forage cap.
2. Eye. *Rouler des calots*, to roll one's eyes.

calotin, e, *sb.m.f.* 1. Priest.
2. Church-goer, person siding with the priests, clerical (disparaging).

calotte, *sb.f.* 1. (*Lit.* skull-cap) Priesthood, black-cattle; friends of priests. *A bas la calotte!* down with the priests! down with clericalism!
2. Box on the ear. *Je vais te donner une calotte*, I am going to slap your face.

camarade, *sb.m.* (From the Germans' cry *Kamerad*.) *Faire camarade*, to give oneself up, to surrender.

camarade-syndiqué, *sb.m.* Term of friendship among workmen whether of the same trade-union or not, 'mate'.

camaro, *sb.f.* (= camarade) Friend. *Les camaros*, pals, chums.

cambouis, *sb.m. Royal cambouis* (= train des equipages), Army Service Corps, soldier belonging to this corps.

cambrio, *sb.m.* (= cambrioleur) Burglar.

cambriole, *sb.f.* 1. Room.
2. Act of *cambrioler* (breaking into a room).
3. Trade of a burglar.

Cambronne, *proper name. Le mot de Cambronne*, the word supposed to have been uttered by General Cambronne at Waterloo when summoned to surrender, *i.e.* MERDE.

cambrousard, *sb.m.* 1. Peasant, clodhopper.
2. Wide-awake fellow.

cambrousse, *sb.f.* Country (opposed to town).

cambuse, *sb.f.* House (usually pejorative). *C'est une cambuse*, it is a beastly hole, a dog-hole.

camelot du roi, *sb.m.* (*Lit.* king's hawker.) Young man affiliated to the *Action française*, a royalist association, and selling royalist papers for propaganda.

camelote, *sb.f.* 1. Worthless stuff, rubbish, junk. *C'est de la camelote*, it's regular trash.
2. Any stuff (good or bad). *Fais voir la camelote!* let us

Discovered in an over-thirty-year-old obscure French to English 1935 dictionary, the word "camaro" was appropriately selected as the name of the new car late in 1966.

PANTHER was the operating code name for the coming new car before CAMARO was announced. Whether by design, or by accident, GM released this artist's sketch of a "Panther" in early 1966.

In April of 1964, Ford Motor Company presented what would become their second successful new car introduction in four years. Following the lead of their highly successful 1960 Falcon, their new Mustang would sell one million units within 12 months and its name would provide the descriptive basis for a whole new type of "pony cars".

Designed to satisfy a market perceived to be young, active, outdoor types with tastes for the more sporty and less conventional, the marketing strategy behind the car included offering a basic model and then encouraging its embellishment by the addition of a myriad of available options.

At the time that the car appeared, despite several design excursions, Chevrolet had no competing automobile. In truth, earliest Mustang dealer training included a comparative analysis of their new car versus the Chevrolet Corvair Monsa, a car with which there really would have been no practical comparison.

It was incumbent upon Chevrolet to respond to what was early correctly perceived to be a challenge to their leadership, and in August of 1964, GM top management gave its approval to the development of a car designed to compete. The parameters would be about the same; perhaps Chevrolet's new car would be a bit larger than the then-existing Mustang, but it too could be expected to grow somewhat in size. The Chevrolet car would sell for about the same price, be about the same size, but would be designed with a wider tread width for better roadability and a slightly larger body shell to offer increased passenger comfort. Beyond that, it would match the developed Ford sales philosophy, which was to offer the inexpensive basic car but encourage the addition of options.

In almost exactly 24 months from the start, the new car appeared in the Dealers' showrooms and they were truly an exciting challenge to Ford. Over 220,000 were sold in their first year (almost ten times the number of Corvettes sold), almost half the total sold by Ford for that year, and their continuity was assured.

A technician, putting finishing touches on a clay model of the coming car appears before styling sketches illustrating some of the many versions considered.

From the time of the go-ahead in the summer of 1966, Chevrolet proceeded with all haste. Basic design characteristics followed the then-existing construction of the Chevy II in which the engine and front suspension became part of a sub-frame which was bolted to a *unitized* frameless body. Thus, by using production Chevy II units as "mules", concepts were evolved and tested while basic design proceeded. Ultimately, many components were shared between the two lines.

Early development model of the 1967 Camaro was used extensively in road testing concepts and components.

Well regarded photograph furnished by Chevrolet showed exploded view of 1967 Sport Coupe with major components all illustrated.

Intriguing cut-away view of 1967 Camaro appeared in popular press as well as in 1967 Camaro sales folder.

SS350 option included not only the visible items, but also the new 350 cubic inch 295 horsepower Turbo-Fire engine which was available only with the SS option.

Presented to the public on September 12, 1966, the 1967 Camaro was eagerly accepted. Following the marketing concept originally agreed upon, the basic Sport Coupe was offered at a low price of only $2466 with its standard six cylinder engine and three speed transmission. Over 80 desirable factory Options were offered though that easily brought the price of delivered cars close to over $3500.

Attractive Sport Coupe for 1967 provided the basis for all subsequent variations.

Helping to establish a youth-oriented affiliation, many of Chervolet's publicity photos for the 1967 Camaro were posed depicting the activities of such people.

In this well known example of creative photography, a heavily retouched photo of an SS350 was later stripped onto a blank billboard before which a Convertible much earlier had been posed. Note that the raised hand appears to be conceptual, and further confusing the issue, the color retouched versions of this photo deleted the Camaro nameplate on the front fender of the convertible.

Design studies are done on a continuing basis at Chevrolet and many of these contain features that are later incorporated into production. Three of the more unusual "dream car" versions of the Camaro are shown here.

1967 Camaro WAIKIKI. Based on a SS350 Convertible, it featured teak wood side panels and wood-bar grille, it also had deep-pile gold carpeting and yellow and okra vinyl seats, and a specially-made trailer hitch and trailer. On its wire wheels were oversized G70 x 15 tires. Its front and rear side-mounted marker lights and its dual rear view mirrors were among items that later appeared on production cars. An interesting feature were the taillamps whose color changed from green to amber to red as they detected the accelerator and the brake pedal.

1968 Camaro CARIBE. This version features a five foot long pickup box with vinyl sidewalls and teak floor planks, hot beverage dispenser in the console, aerodynamic roll bar, and 15 inch aluminum wheels with wide oval tires having brushed aluminum inserts. More unique features were a front air intake containing small high intensity lamps, rear-mounted lamps which flashed at high frequency to provide unusually effective stop signals, and a headerless windshield.

1978 Camaro BERLINETTA. In addition to an extended front cap featuring a wide integrated bumper and deeply recessed headlamps, the car displayed unusual graphics on its safety-pinned hood.

1967 Chevrolet Camaro SS Convertible, Official Pace Car for the Indianapolis 500 Mile Race held that year on July 30th.

Selection as the Pace Car at the Indy race each year is an honor eagerly sought after. Many newly-introduced cars especially seek the assignment due to the increased exposure that results. While the actual Pace Car is almost always a specially prepared version, "replicas", or similarly decorated, models are frequently made available.

The attractive white 1967 Pace Car, with attractive blue custom interior and boot, and blue front header stripe was no exception. No records exist to confirm, but it is generally believed that about 100 of these replicas were manufactured.

Photo courtesy Indianapolis Motor Speedway Corporation

The Z28, due to its larger seating capacity, became the "Official Car" (not to be confused with the "Pace Car") in 1978 when the Corvette held that honor. Several were engaged as festival and press vehicles.

In 1978, several Camaro Z28 Sport Coupes were selected by the California Highway Patrol to be tested as law enforcement vehicles. Most were assigned to the heavily trafficed Southern California corridor between Fresno and El Centro. Well-liked by drivers, these cars were later phased out due to several factors. Among them were seating limitations; transportation of prisoners was a major problem!

The 1980 Camaro ULTRA Z is another styling exercise performed as a variation on the Z28. Boasting a turbo-charged engine and a Cararra-inspired rear spoiler, it possesed, in addition to its removable top panels, some outstandingly attractive graphics.

1982 Camaro Sport Coupe

The 1981 Camaro marked the end of the line for a basic body style that had endured since 1979. The intervening years dictated a need for change and Chevrolet responded. An increasing need for better fuel economy dictated a downsizing to reduce weight, and a new car was first spotted on road tests in the Fall of 1980! It was an attractive car, some six inches or so shorter than the 1981 model. With a wheelbase decreased by about 7 inches, although the tread width and height remained about the same, its interior dimensions seemed essentially unchanged. With the emphasis placed on weight reduction, the 1982 Camaro would prove to be about 600 pounds lighter than its predecessor. This brilliant new Camaro was also destined to be the first of its line to offer as standard a new four cylinder engine although optional V-8 engines were still to be offered.

Look at that! ➝ ·

That's a Camaro Sport Coupe. This is how it comes.
Strato-bucket seats, a pair. Full carpeting. Vinyl
interior. Wide-stance wheels for flatter cornering.
A 3-speed transmission, fully synchronized. A 140-hp
Six that hates to stop for gas. And a lengthy list of
new safety features, including the GM-developed

energy-absorbing steering column, dual master cylinder
brake system with warning light, folding front seat
back latches, four-way hazard warning flasher.
    There. Now you start adding extra-cost options. If it
suits your style, order Camaro with Rally Sport equipment
(hideaway headlights, special trim) and the Custom

Command Performance

GM

Look at this: ⟶ $2466⁰⁰

Interior. For more excitement, there's SS 350 gear: 295-hp V8, louver-styled hood, bold striping; then add front disc brakes, a 4-speed and like that. As for comforts, ask for the Strato-back front seat, stereo tape system, even air conditioning. Make Camaro *your* idea of a car at your Chevrolet dealer's now!

Manufacturer's suggested retail price for Camaro Sport Coupe (Model 12337). To this price add options shown in illustration—style trim group, $40.05; wheel covers, $21.10; and whitewall tires, $31.35. All prices include Federal Excise Tax and suggested dealer delivery and handling charge (transportation charges, accessories, other optional equipment, state and local taxes additional).

CHEVROLET

For '67, everything new that could happen... happened!

Camaro
The Chevrolet you've been waiting for

25

In this, among the first of the "Hugger" ads in which Chevy sought to extoll the handling characteristics of the Camaro, the floor-shift transmission and hood stripe were additional no-cost inducements.

Reproduced here in black & white, the red-line tires shown in the original color ad are not apparent. "Red Lines" were heavily promoted during this period as badges on the performance cars.

Try Camaro—"The Hugger"

Camaro hugs a road closer, straightens a curve easier because it's the
widest stance sportster at its price. It's lower, heavier, too . . . big-car solid and steady.
You get a better ride, more precise handling for your money.
Ask any Camaro owner, he'll tell you.

Now, during the Camaro Pacesetter Sale,
you also get special savings on specially equipped sport coupes and convertibles.
Save on all this: the 250-cu.-in. Six,
whitewalls, wheel covers, bumper guards, wheel-opening moldings, body striping,
deluxe steering wheel, extra brightwork inside.
And, at no extra cost during the Sale,
get a floor shift for the 3-speed transmission and the sporty hood stripe!
Compare Camaro. See your Chevrolet dealer now.
(Sale savings, too, on specially equipped Fleetside pickups, Model C5 10934.)

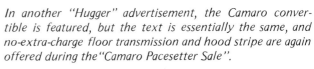

CAMARO
by Chevrolet

*In another "Hugger" advertisement, the Camaro conver-
tible is featured, but the text is essentially the same, and
no-extra-charge floor transmission and hood stripe are again
offered during the "Camaro Pacesetter Sale".*

*GM's AC Spark Plug Division obtained some ancillary bene-
fit by this advertisement which tied their product in to the
new 1967 Camaro.*

This attractive advertisement appears in the center-fold of the 1967 Indianapolis 500 official race Program. In it, the 1967 Official Pace Car is displayed complete with blue hood and body stripes and red line tires.

Look what's setting the pace its first year out!
CAMARO

Picked by the pros

Lots of other people are picking it,
really sets the pace. First glance p
wider, heavier. Roomier, too. First r
and stability. Wide new stance do
also leads with more of what leave
— 210 hp. More cubes in the stan

Compare CAMARO...to le

- 56 -

Drawing on their identification as the 1967 Indianapolis Pace Car, Chevy offered the special hood stripe (and a floor-mounted shifter) at no extra charge during a special "pacesetter" sale.

lianapolis 500 Pace Car

se who want a smooth sure-handling car that
naro the frontrunner in sporty looks: lower,
it's the pacesetter for sports-car handling
nother exclusive at Camaro's price. Camaro
ers behind. More power in the standard V8
— 230.

hy it gives you that sure feeling.

- 57 -

1967 *Here at last was Chevrolet's answer to the Mustang! Offered at a deceptively low $2,466, few were actually delivered at that level. Transportation charges, accessories, other optional equipment, and state and local taxes added hundreds of dollars to the total.*

The 1967 Camaro was offered in 15 exterior colors:

AA	Tuxedo Black	GG	Granada Gold	NN	Maderia Maroon
CC	Ermine White	HH	Mountain Green (medium)	RR	Bolero Red
DD	Nantucket Blue (medium)	KK	Emerald Turquoise (medium)	SS	Sierra Fawn
EE	Deepwater Blue (dark)	LL	Tahoe Turquoise (dark)	TT	Capri Cream
FF	Marina Blue (bright)	MM	Royal Plum	YY	Butternut Yellow

Safety was a major consideration by 1967. Ralph Nader had brought the subject into focus with his book *Unsafe at any Speed* and in the ensuing events, GM had come out looking badly. Accordingly, their new cars for 1967, the last before the Government took a major interest in the matter, had many features that were worth trumpeting. Among the many safety-related items for the new Camaro were: dual master brake cylinder with warning light, energy-absorbing steering column and instrument panel (which also featured smoothly contoured knobs and levers), break-away rear view mirror, low profile window control knobs, seat belts, both front and rear, padded sun visors, front seat-back latches, standard outside rear view mirror, back-up lights, etc.

Camaro SS : One to go, with everything.

CHEVROLET Camaro

1967 CAMARO POWER TEAM CHART

Engine Bore and Stroke	Equipment Compression Ratio	Transmission	Axle Ratio Std.	Axle Ratio Opt.	
Standard Engines					
140-hp Turbo-Thrift 230 3.875″ x 3.25″	1-Bbl. Carb. Hydraulic lifters 8.5:1	3-Speed (2.85:1 Low) 4-Speed (3.11:1 Low)	3.08:1	2.73:1 3.55:1	
		Powerglide	2.73:1	3.55:1	
210-hp Turbo-Fire 327 4.00″ x 3.25″	2-Bbl. Carb. Hydraulic lifters 8.75:1	3-Speed (2.54:1 Low) 4-Speed (2.54:1 Low)	3.08:1	2.73:1 3.55:1	
		Powerglide	2.73:1	3.55:1	
Extra-cost Engines					
155-hp Turbo-Thrift 250 3.875″ x 3.53″	1-Bbl. Carb. Hydraulic lifters 8.5:1	3-Speed (2.85:1 Low) 4-Speed (3.11:1 Low)	3.08:1	2.73:1 3.55:1	
		Powerglide	2.73:1	3.55:1	
275-hp Turbo-Fire 327 4.00″ x 3.25″	4-Bbl. Carb. Hydraulic lifters 10.0:1	3-Speed (2.54:1 Low) 4-Speed (2.54:1 Low)	3.08:1	2.73:1 3.55:1	
		Powerglide	2.73:1	3.55:1	
295-hp Turbo-Fire 350 4.00″ x 3.48″	4-Bbl. Carb. Hydraulic lifters 10.25:1	3-Speed (2.54:1 Low)	3.31:1	3.07:1 3.55:1	
		Special 3-Speed (2.41:1 Low) 4-Speed (2.52:1 Low)	3.31:1	3.07:1 3.55:1 3.73:1	4.10:1† 4.56:1† 4.88:1†
		Powerglide	3.31:1	3.07:1 3.55:1 3.73:1	

†Positraction required. Positraction may be specified with all other ratios.

Other standard features on the new Camaro included black-grid front grille, single-unit headlights and parking direction lights mounted in the grille, windshield reveal molding, rear window reveal molding in the Sport Coupes, front fender nameplates, body sill moldings, taillights with built-in back-up lights, bright metal hub caps, Strato-Bucket front seats, all-vinyl interior trim, embossed vinyl door and sidewall trim panels, front arm rests, foam-cushioned front seats, oval steering wheel with horn button, deep-twist floor carpeting, oil pressure, temperature, and generator warning lights.

SPECIFICATIONS
Wheelbase—108.0″ Overall length—184.7″ Overall width—72.5″ Overall height—51.4″ Road clearance (min.)—5.5″ Tread (base wheels and tires): front—59.0″; rear—58.9″ Turning diameter: curb to curb—38.5′ Fuel tank capacity—18 gals. approx.

Dimensions (in.)		Sport Coupe	Convertible
Headroom	Front	37.7	37.6
	Rear	36.5	36.8
Leg Room	Front	42.5	42.5
	Rear	29.9	29.6
Hip Room	Front	56.3	56.3
	Rear	54.5	47.5
Shoulder Room	Front	56.7	56.7
	Rear	53.8	47.3
Entrance Height	Front	29.3	29.3
Luggage Compartment			
Loading Height		30.0	30.0
Total Volume (cu. ft.)		19.6	17.4
Usable Luggage Space (cu. ft.)		8.3	5.6
Curb Weight (lb.)	(6)	2910	3165
	(V8)	3070	3325

1967

Sport Coupe:
Model 12337-SIX
Model 12437-V8

Convertible:
Model 12367-SIX
Model 12467-V8

Regular Production Options (RPO) are those variations from the basic model that are offered, provided, and installed at the factory. Differing from Custom Feature Accessories installed by the Dealers, (next page), they included, on introduction of the 1967 Camaro, those listed on this page.

Camaro features

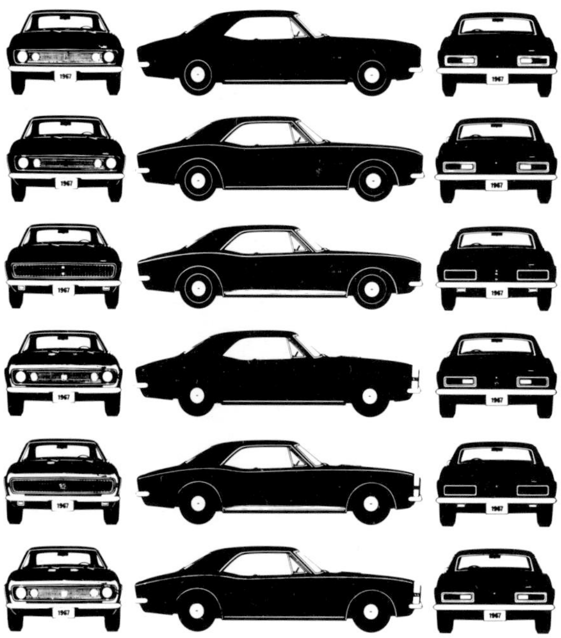

CAMARO / *Sport Coupe / Convertible*

Distinctive black-grid grille with emblem • Grille opening molding • Single-unit headlights with anodized aluminum bezels • Grille-mounted parking and directional signals • Windshield reveal molding • Front panel nameplate • Body sill moldings • Camaro fender identification emblem • Front fender engine identification emblem (V8 or extra-cost six only) • Bright metal hub caps • Bright ventipane frames • Chrome outside rearview mirror • Bright bezel dual-unit rear lights with built-in backup lights • Rear window reveal molding (sport coupe) • Deck lid nameplate.

CAMARO / *Style Trim*

Style Trim Group (RPO Z21) is available at extra cost for standard Camaro models and includes these distinctive bright accents:

Front and rear wheel opening moldings • Body side accent stripes • Roof drip cap moldings (sport coupe only).

CAMARO / *Rally Sport*

Rally Sport option (RPO Z22) offers the following special features (including Style Trim Group—RPO Z21) in addition to or replacing standard Camaro equipment:

Special full-width black-grid grille with headlights concealed behind power-operated covers • Front valance panel-mounted parking and directional signal lights • RS center grille emblem • Front and rear wheel opening moldings • Body side accent stripes • Lower body side moldings • Bright roof drip cap molding (coupe only) • RS front fender emblem • Special black-accented rear light bezels • RS fuel cap and emblem • Rear valance panel-mounted backup lights.

CAMARO / *SS 350*

SS 350 option (RPO L48) includes the following special features in addition to or replacing standard Camaro equipment:

295-hp Turbo-Fire 350 V8 • Special hood with raised center area, simulated louvers and extra-thick underhood insulation • Color-keyed paint band and striping around grille • SS 350 grille emblem • SS front fender emblems • SS 350 fuel filler cap emblem • Special red-stripe nylon tires with 6" wheels plus special engine and chassis components.

CAMARO / *Rally Sport SS 350*

Camaro models can also be ordered with the Rally Sport option (RPO Z22) in combination with SS 350 equipment (RPO L48) to include all the special features of both (except that RS emblems are replaced with SS or SS 350 identification).

CAMARO / *SS 350 Style Trim*

Both SS 350 option (RPO L48) and Style Trim Group (RPO Z21) can be ordered in combination with each other. This combination includes all the features of both options as listed above.

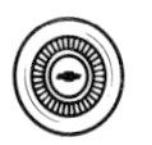

Hub caps—standard on all models

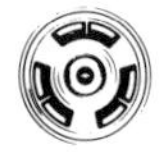

Wheel covers—on order for all models

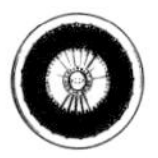

Simulated wire wheel covers—on order for all models

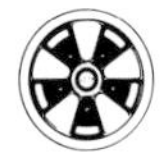

Mag-style wheel covers—on order for all models

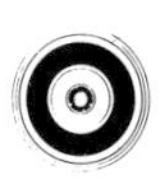

Special wheel trim with extra-cost front disc brakes

SS 350

350-cu.-in. V8 engine identification (included with SS 350 option)

Camaro

SPORT COUPE 4-PASSENGER
MODEL 12337—SIX
MODEL 12437—V8

CONVERTIBLE 4-PASSENGER
MODEL 12367—SIX
MODEL 12467—V8

EXTERIOR FEATURES

Windshield pillar and rear belt moldings on convertible.
Slender body sill moldings.
Black plastic grille.
Single-unit headlights.
Grille-mounted parking lights.
Bright metal hub caps.
Taillights with bright bezels and built-in backup lights.
Weather-resistant vinyl-coated fabric top with manual operation on convertible.

INTERIOR FEATURES

Luxurious color-keyed all-vinyl upholstery.
Strato-bucket front seats.
Fold-down rear seat can be ordered.
Scuff-resistant plastic cowl side panels with molded-in ventilator grilles.
Color-keyed deep-twist carpeting.
Front armrests with bright bases.
Built-in rear armrests in convertible.
Cigarette lighter; built-in ashtray in instrument panel.
Dual courtesy lights in convertible.
Automatic front door switches for dome or courtesy lights; also manual control on instrument panel.
Locking glove compartment; friction-type ventipanes.
Conventional rear seat with bucket styling.

CAMARO RALLY SPORT (RPO Z22—includes special features of Style Trim Group)
Special features replacing standard equipment
Distinctive parking lights below front bumper.
Special grille with headlights concealed behind electrically operated panels.
"rs" grille, fender and gas cap emblems.
Wide lower body moldings.
Front and rear wheel opening moldings.
Roof drip gutter moldings on coupe.
Body side accent stripes.
Black-painted taillight bezels.
Backup lights below rear bumper.

STYLE TRIM GROUP (RPO Z21)
Special features replacing standard equipment
Front and rear wheel opening moldings.
Roof drip gutter moldings on coupe.
Body side accent stripes.

CAMARO SS 350 (RPO L48)
Special features replacing standard equipment
295-hp Turbo-Fire 350 V8.
"SS" grille, fender and gas cap emblems.
Special hood and ornaments.
Distinctive front hood stripes.
Special red-stripe tires.

SPECIAL INTERIOR GROUP (RPO Z23)
Special features replacing standard equipment
Bright pedal pad frames.
Windshield pillar moldings in bright metal.
Roof rail moldings in coupe.

CUSTOM INTERIOR (RPO Z87)
Special features replacing standard equipment
Roof rear quarter dome lights on sport coupe.
Recessed door handles.
Color-keyed accent bands on front and rear seats.
Special front armrests.
Glove compartment light.
Three-spoke oval steering wheel with ornaments.
Carpeted scuff panels on doors.
Molded luggage compartment mat.
Strato-back front seat with fold-down center armrest may be specified in place of Strato-bucket seats.

OPTIONAL FEATURES†	RPO
Axle, Positraction Rear	G80
POWER ASSISTS	
Brakes, Power	J50
Steering, Power	N40
Windows, Power	A31
FEATURE GROUPS	
(All items in Groups may be ordered separately.)	
Appearance Guard Group—Front and rear floor mats, front bumper guards, custom deluxe seat belts, door edge guards, rear bumper guards.	
Auxiliary Lighting Group—Includes the following when not standard: glove compartment light, courtesy lights, underhood light, ashtray light, luggage light.	
Foundation Group—AM pushbutton radio, electric clock.	
Operating Convenience Group—Outside remote-control mirror, rear window defroster (except convertible).	
EXTERIOR FEATURES	
Guards, Door Edge	B93
Guards, Front Bumper	V31
Guards, Rear Bumper	V32
Mirror, Outside Remote Control	D33
Roof Cover, Vinyl (Black or beige)	C08
Top, Convertible (White, black or blue)	
Manual	C05
Power	C05/C06
Wheel Covers	P01
Wheel Covers, Mag-style	N96
Wheel Covers, Simulated Wire	P02
INTERIOR FEATURES	
Air Conditioning, Four-Season	C60
Belts, Front Shoulder	
With standard seat belts	AS1
With custom deluxe seat belts	A85
Clock, Electric	U35
Console, Center	D55
Defroster, Rear Window	C50
Glass, Soft-Ray Tinted—All windows	A01
Windshield only	A02
Harness, Shoulder	A85
Headrests, Strato-ease—Front seat	AS2
Instrumentation, Special—Includes tachometer, electric clock, ammeter, temperature and oil pressure gauges (with V8s only)	U17
Lights	
Ashtray	U28
Courtesy	U29
Glove compartment	U27
Luggage compartment	U25
Underhood	U26
Mats, Floor/Front (2) and Rear (2)	B37
Radios, Pushbutton—with front antenna	
AM Radio	U63
AM Radio and Rear Seat Speaker	U63/U80
AM-FM Radio	U69
AM-FM Radio and Rear Seat Speaker	U69/U80
Antenna, Rear Manual	U73
Seat Belts, Custom Deluxe (color-matched)	A39
Seat, Fold-down Rear	A67
Seat, Strato-back	AL4
Speed Control, Cruise-Master	K30
Speed Warning Indicator	U15
Steering Wheel, Comfortilt	N33
Steering Wheel, Deluxe	N30
Steering Wheel, Sports-styled	N34
Stereo Tape System	U57
HEAVY-DUTY AND OTHER EQUIPMENT	
Battery, Heavy-Duty	T60
Brake Linings, Sintered-Metallic	J65
Brakes, Front Disc	J52
Engine Ventilation, Closed Positive-Type	K24
Exhaust System, Deep-Note Dual	N61
Exhaust System, Dual	N10
Fan, Temperature-Controlled	K02
Generators, Delcotron	
12-42-Ampere	K79
Heater-Defroster Deletion	C48
Horn, Tri-Volume	U03
Radiator, Heavy-Duty	V01
Steering, Special	N44
Suspension, Special-Purpose Front and Rear	F41
Wheels, 14" with 6JK Rims	P12

†Availability and application determined by model or other equipment.

POWER TEAMS

Engine	3-Speed Fully Synch.	Special 3-Speed Fully Synch.	4-Speed Fully Synch.	Power-glide
Standard 140-hp Turbo-Thrift 230 (230-cu.-in. 6)	Standard		RPO M20	RPO M35
Standard 210-hp Turbo-Fire 327 (327-cu.-in. V8)	Standard		RPO M20	RPO M35
RPO L22 155-hp Turbo-Thrift 250 (250-cu.-in. 6)	Standard		RPO M20	RPO M35
RPO L30 275-hp Turbo-Fire 327 (327-cu.-in. V8)	Standard		RPO M20	RPO M35
RPO L48 295-hp Turbo-Fire 350 (350-cu.-in. V8) (Included with SS 350 only)	Standard	RPO M13	RPO M20	RPO M35

Camaro

INTERIOR FEATURES & APPOINTMENTS

INSTRUMENT PANEL	CAMARO (CUSTOM INTERIOR)	CAMARO (SPECIAL INTERIOR GROUP)	CAMARO
Black textured-finish instrument cluster facing with bright molding	•	•	•
Bright rimmed instrument bezels	•	•	•
Oil pressure, temperature and generator warning lights	•	•	•
Parking brake and brake system warning light	•	•	•
Color-keyed turn signal and shift lever knobs	•	•	•
Large-diameter bright control knobs	•	•	•
Cigarette lighter	•	•	•
Electric clock	EC	EC	EC
Painted glove compartment door	•	•	•
Glove compartment lock	•	•	•
Glove compartment light	•	EC	EC
DOORS & SIDE PANELS			
Molded vinyl door trim with carpeted panel	•		
Vinyl door and/or sidewall trim panels		•	•
Scuff-resistant plastic cowl side panels	•	•	•
Friction-type ventipanes	•	•	•
Front door armrests (molded in Camaro Custom Interior)	•	•	•
Rear armrests with built-in ashtrays	•	Conv.	Conv.
SEATS			
Strato-bucket front seats	•	•	•
All-vinyl seat trim (special design with Custom Interior)	•	•	•
Foam-cushioned front seat	•	•	•
Fold-down rear seat	EC	EC	EC
HEADLINING, FLOOR COVERING & INTERIOR FEATURES			
Embossed vinyl headlining	•	•	•
Padded sun visors	•	•	•
Color-keyed deep-twist floor carpeting	•	•	•
Day-night rearview mirror with cushioned frame	•	•	•
Bright windshield header (convertible only)	•	•	•
Bright windshield pillar moldings		•	
Bright roof rail moldings (sport coupe only)		•	
Bright pedal pad trim		•	
Color-keyed plastic coat hooks (sport coupe only)	•	•	•

LUGGAGE COMPARTMENT	CAMARO (CUSTOM INTERIOR)	CAMARO (SPECIAL INTERIOR GROUP)	CAMARO
Molded rubber luggage compartment mat	•		
Spatter-painted luggage compartment	•	•	•
LIGHTS, SWITCHES & POWER EQUIPMENT			
Four-way hazard flasher system switch on steering column	•	•	•
Interior light switch (in headlight switch)	•	•	•
Automatic front door courtesy or dome light switches	•	•	•
Roof rear quarter lights (sport coupe only)	•		
Center dome light with bright bezel (except convertible)		•	•
Dual instrument panel courtesy lights (EC on sport coupe)	Conv.	Conv.	Conv.
Convertible power-operated folding top	EC	EC	EC

EC—Extra cost.

SAFETY ITEMS INCLUDED IN EVERY NEW CAMARO
Dual master cylinder brake system with warning light • Energy-absorbing steering column • Energy-absorbing instrument panel with smooth contoured knobs and levers • Padded instrument panel • Lane-change feature incorporated in direction signal control • Inside day-night mirror with shatter-resistant vinyl-edged glass and breakaway support • Soft, low profile window control knobs, and coat hooks • Seat belts, front and rear, with pushbutton buckles • Front seat belt retractors • Front seat shoulder belt anchors • Padded sun visors • Passenger-guard door locks—all doors • Folding front seat back latches • Four-way hazard warning flasher • Energy-absorbing steering wheel • Thick-laminate windshield • Dual-speed windshield wipers • Windshield washer • Reduced-glare instrument panel and windshield wiper arms and blades • Outside rearview mirror • Backup lights • Uniform Powerglide shift quadrant (PRNDL) • Safety door latches and hinges • Tire safety rim • Corrosion-resistant brake lines.

PLUS THESE IMPORTANT CAMARO FEATURES
Big car power and stability • Trim, sporty silhouette; roomy interiors • Fresh new long-hood, short-deck styling concept • Quality Body by Fisher • Magic-Mirror acrylic lacquer finish • High-level ventilation system • Built-in blended-air heater-defroster system • Friction-type ventipanes • High-mounted independent spring front suspension • Statically balanced wheels and tires • Self-adjusting air-cooled Safety-Master brakes • Ball-Race steering gear • Battery-saving Delcotron generator • Delco energizer battery • Front and rear fender inner skirts for rust prevention • Flush-and-dry rocker panels • Long-life exhaust system.

	1965 Ford Mustang	1967 Ford Mustang	1967 CAMARO
Overall length inches	181.6	183.6	184.7
Height inches	51.1	51.6	51.0
Width inches	68.2	70.9	72.5
Wheelbase inches	108	108	108
Weight lbs.	2562	2695	2912

EXTERIOR DIMENSIONS (sport coupe)

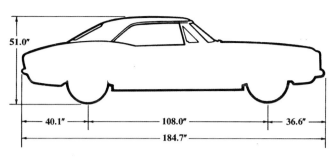

INTERIOR DIMENSIONS (sport coupe)

	Front	Rear
Head room	37.7″	36.7″
Leg room	42.5″	29.9″
Shoulder room	56.7″	53.8″
Usable luggage capacity (cu. ft.)		8.3

In addition to the factory-installed Options, there were many "Custom Feature Accessories" available from the Dealer for the new Camaro. These authorized Dealer-added items included the following:

GM Chevrolet air conditioner	contour rubber floor mats
Vanity visor mirror	highway emergency kit
rear window defroster	front and rear bumper guards
tissue dispenser	ventilated seat cushions
deluxe AM-FM radio and antenna	tri-volume horn
Delco stereo tape player	spare tire lock
push button radio and antenna	temperature modulated fan
manual tuned radio and antenna	fire extinguisher
stereo multiplex	locking gas cap
rear seat speaker	door edge guards
cruise-master speed control	stainless wheelcovers
power brakes	magnesium-type full wheel covers
front seat belt retractors	wire wheel covers
electric clock	courtesy lights
auto compass	hand portable spot light
tachometer (dash mounted)	litter container (two types)
rear deck luggage carrier	underhood light
ski rack	luggage compartment light
ash tray light	glove compartment light

Camaro

custom feature accessories for '67

1967 CAMARO Sport Coupe

Careful observation of the 1967 hood and deck-lid insignia reveals that it is actually composed of two separate pieces.

Mr. John Dugan, Oceanside, California

35

Standard 1967 Camaro front end is distinctive with two round parking/directional signal lamps placed inboard of the headlamps.

Full-width chromed steel bumper wraps protectively around front corner.

Additional openings below the front bumper allow cooling air entry. Front license support, attaches to lower front valance panel.

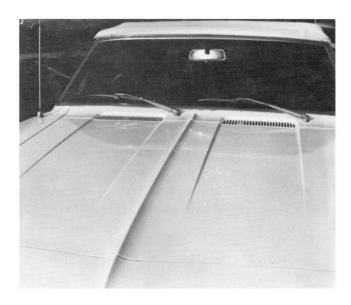

This basic hood is used on all 1967-69 Camaros except for the large-engine versions.

A stylized emblem appears at the center of the grille.

On 1967 models, "Camaro" is subordinate to "Chevrolet".

The blacked-out egg crate front grill emphasises the appearance of the parking lights.

Single-bulb sealed beam headlamps are surrounded with bright metal trim.

These emblems appear both on the front of the hood and also on the rear deck lid.

Camaro's unique hood has long flowing longitudinal creases that emphasise the appearance of the air intake grills.

Wheel openings are somewhat semi-circular in appearance.

Mirror is suspended from windshield top frame on a bracket designed to give way under impact. Note padding of bracket mount.

One piece wrap-around windshield flows well into rooflines.

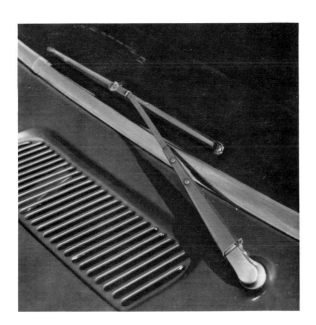

Dual-speed wipers are standard as are windshield washers.

Camaro nameplate is standard on sides of fenders. Selection of one of the optional V-8 engines results in addition of engine size and V-8 insignia in addition.

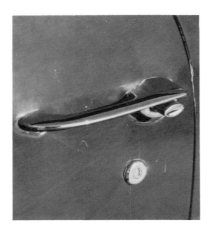

Outside door handles are chromed, pushbutton type.

Owner has added the side rub rail, an accessory that becomes increasingly popular well into the 70's.

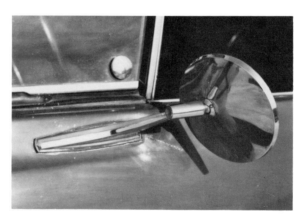

1967 Camaro is distinctive for its use of vent windows which only appeared on that year's models.

The round outside rear view mirror is standard for this year.

The vehicles Identification Number (VIN), is stamped on a plate riveted to the left side door post.

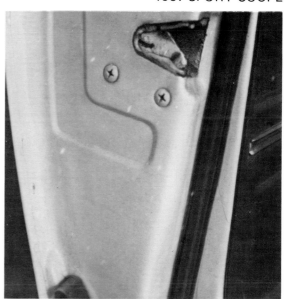

Door jambs are embossed for strength.

Metallic decals are used on the trailing door edges both as an advertisement and also a reflected warning to oncoming traffic.

Lower body is embossed with distinctive crease, and a straight rocker panel trim strip provided for emphasis.

Aluminum scuff plates are used on the sill beneath the doors.

The Fisher body logo appears on the scuff plates at the entry.

Large one-piece rear window gives good visibility.

Rear deck lid opens to provide access to luggage storage space stated to be as much as 8.3 cubic feet.

Standard tire is size 7.35-14 in blackwall. Optional upgradings include same in whitewall or size D70-14 red stripe.

Lenses of the taillamps are patterned to increase intensity of lights.

Taillamps include both red marker and stop functions, and also white standard back up light.

Rear view of car emphasises the clean uncluttered look.

Rear bumper guards are an option offered by the factory.

The rear bumper also wraps protectively around the fender.

1967 Camaro Convertible

The Convertible model appeared to be losing favor in the mid-sixties, and annual production figures support the fact that sales were declining. In introducing this new model in 1967, Chevrolet must certainly have gambled greatly as tooling was of no inconsequential cost. There were only 25,141 of these attractive cars built in 1967, the highest total of any Camaro convertible, yet still only about ten percent of the year's total production.

Mr. Henry Velasco, San Diego, California

Convertible greatly resembles the Sport Coupe from this view.

Canvas top mates smoothly with windshield header to provide clean flowing lines.

Convertible tops were offered in 1967 in white, blue, or black.

The standard hood is shared with the Sport Coupe.

Lower body sides of the Convertible have same embossment as does Sport Coupe (page 41), and again, the bright metal trim strip dresses up this area.

The convertible's folding top is latched to the windshield header which in turn is protected by bright metal bezels.

To allow for the differing construction at point where the folding top front bow and the windshield header join, the convertible's windshield has been shortened by about one inch, thus it will not interchange with that on the Sport Coupe.

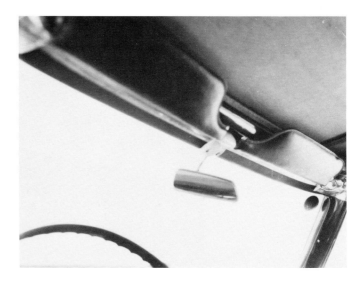

Dual padded sun visors are included as standard equipment.

As in the Sport Coupe, the Convertible features vent wings in the front windows which are rotated to open.

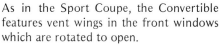

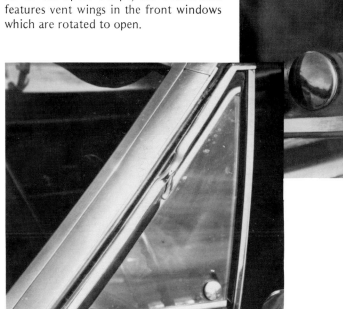

Vent wings are secured by a bright-metal latch.

The large clear vinyl rear window is sewn in place and cannot be opened.

Plastic latches are provided to secure lowered top when power operation option is not ordered.

The deck lid for the Convertible is same as Sport Coupe.

1967 RALLY SPORT

1967 Sport Coupe with Rally Sport option

1967 Convertible with Rally Sport Option *Allan Vanderlind, Loma Vista, California*

Front bumper is the same but Rally Sport option places parking/directional lamps below.

Although including other items as well, the Rally Sport option's most obvious feature is the full-width grill with its concealed headlamp system.

Distinctive RS grill emblem is featured on grille.

Rectangular parking lamps are chrome-framed.

Distinctive RS emblem appears on front fenders.

The Rally Sport option is essentially an appearance dress-up. In addition to the concealed headlamp system, it also provides RS emblems on the grill and fuel filler cap, lower body side molding, body accent stripes, the rectangular parking/turning lamps shown opposite, backup lamps below the rear bumper, bright metal front and rear wheel opening moldings, and an RS emblem on the steering wheel. It can be ordered with either the Sport Coupe or with the Convertible.

Concealed headlamp system is achieved by rotating a matching plate in front of the lamps. Electric motors under the hood are activated by the headlamp switch on the dashboard.

RS emblem appears at hub of steering wheel.

Special RS fuel filler cap is supplied.

A distinctively shaped bright metal lower body side molding is included in the Rally Sport option.

Unlike "regular" 1967 taillight (page 43) which includes a backup light, the rally sport rear lamp has two red segments.

Special rectangular rally sport backup lamp is placed beneath the rear bumper.

Distincitve rear view is highlighted by the RS fuel filler cap and separate backup lights below bumper.

The 1967 optional SS package includes a special hood with the attached ornaments, front header panel paint stripe, underhood insulation, size D70-14 red stripe tires on 14 x 6.00 wheels, suspension features, and SS emblems on radiator grille, fenders, and fuel filler cap. It was available on both Sport Coupe and also Convertible models, and could be ordered separately or in addition to the Rally Sport option. Initially offered only with the 350 engine

(350SS), in March of 1967 the SS package became available with the larger 396 cubic inch engine.

This new option (RPO L35) called for a front fender 396 emblem, other items such as larger capacity radiator, larger fuel lines, heavy duty engine mounts, dual exhaust, heavy duty clutch, special springs and shock absorbers, heavy duty rear axle, and red stripe wide oval tires on 6" wide rims, as well as a blackpainted rear end panel.

1967 SS 350 Camaro Sport Coupe

1967 SS

Harry & Charlotte Bokker, San Diego, California

SS350 was available either *with* the Rally Sport option as shown here, or on standard Camaro front end (page 36). In either case, the SS emblem would prevail.

1967 concealed headlamp doors were operated by electric motors (right) placed under the hood.

The SS350 front end differs little from that of Rally Sport except for grille emblem and exclusive front header panel stripe. Popularity of this unique stripe forced Chevrolet to make it generally available on *any* Camaro starting early in 1967.

SS350 grille emblem was used only with that engine and only in 1967. A one-piece item, it bolted through the grille.

Front header panel strip breaks above and below SS emblems, and runs down until almost concealed by the bumper.

The concealed headlamps and rectangular parking lamps beneath the bumper are actually a part of the Rally Sport option; SS option appeared on standard Camaros as well.

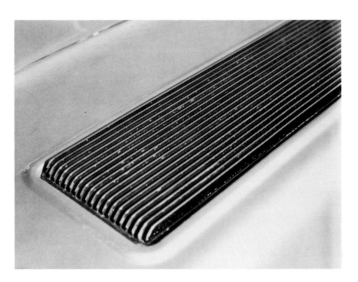

A polished metal casting is used to simulate cooling louvres; originally planned as functional, they remain decorative only due to leakage problems encountered.

The unique "louvred" hood is used only on SS models for 1967.

Although hood differs from standard, the cool air intake chamber is unchanged.

Contrasting hood header panel strip sets off appearance of the two-piece 1967 Chevrolet Camaro insignia on the hood.

Tinted glass in windshield can be ordered separately or with all windows.

The bright metal hub of windshield wiper arm presses on shaft.

Painted lower body rocker panel appears beneath the unique bright metal lower trim strip.

Ordering one of the optional radios results automatically in the necessary antenna being supplied. If rear-mounted antenna was desired, it had to be ordered separately.

Appropriately identified V-8 engines are indicated by insignia on fender flanks.

The distinctively shaped lower body molding is a part of the RS option, not otherwise included in the SS group.

1967 SS

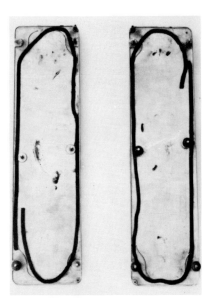

Underside of bright metal "louvres" on hood show gasket required to avoid water collection.

SS option includes under-hood insulation blanket.

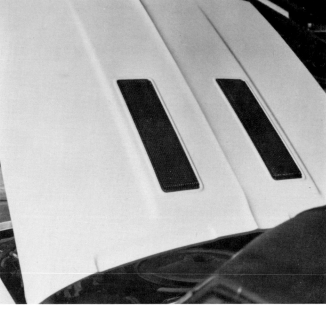

The hood in all Camaros are hinged at the rear; open from the front.

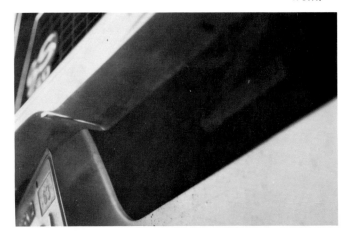

1967 hood release latch is operated by moving handle behind grille.

The vinyl roof cover is not part of the SS option, but is a separate dress-up option. Available only in black or beige.

The optional vinyl roof cover is cemented to the steel roof of the Sport Coupe. It is not available on the Convertible.

Vinyl roof cover runs down the windshield pillars.

The bright metal trim strip at the base of the optional vinyl roof cover is supplied as a part of that option.

Front and rear wheel opening lip moldings are a part of the RS option with which this SS350 is also equipped.

The SS fuel filler cap appears here on a typical Rally Sport rear end as the car is so equipped; if it were not, the SS cap would merely replace the standard cap in the standard rear end.

The two-piece emblem appears again on the rear deck lid.

A polished SS horn button appears at the center of the steering wheel.

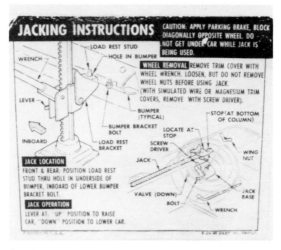

Jacking instruction decals appear on the underside of rear deck lid.

SS and RS fuel filler caps are secured to car with a wire bail unlike the free standing standard caps.

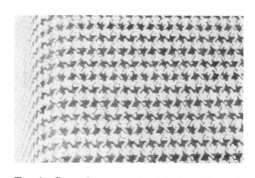

Bright metal bezels surround RS backup lights.

Rear deck lid allows access to luggage compartment said to be 8.3 cubic feet.

Trunk floor is covered with houndstooth grey-and-black protective mat.

Standard four-way flasher hazard warning switch is located below steering wheel on right.

Bright metal escutcheons label WIPER and IGNITION switches.

Cowl-intake air is ducted to outlets on instrument panel.

Turn signal lever is placed below steering wheel on left.

Adjustable chromed outlet directs air flow.

CAMARO appears on horn button unless RS or SS optioned.

Ignition switch is located on panel.

An additional air intake on cowl panel is controlled by sliding switch.

The standard transmission 3-speed shift lever or optional Power-glide automatic lever is placed on the steering column. The floor-mounted 4-speed optional transmission is placed between the seats. One option permitted the 3-speed to be furnished with a floor shifter, but a more popular option was the center console installation which includes the floor shifter as shown here.

Powerglide was the automatic transmission offered with all engines except the 302 and 396 HP versions. The former came standard with 4-speed only, the latter with 3-speed *or* 4-speed. The heavy-duty Turbo Hydra-Matic automatic transmission was also offered as an Option with the Hydraulic-lifter-equipped 396 engine, but not with the mechanical lifter version.

Suspended brake (and clutch, where applicable) pedals were provided with protective rubber pads.

Four-speed floor-mounted transmission is shown with optional console and gauges, but was available separately. Its shift pattern is indicated on its standard black plastic knob.

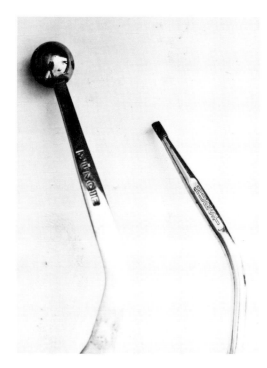

A suspended foot pedal, complete with lettered pad, operates the parking brakes. Release is obtained by pulling the lettered knob just under the instrument panel.

Four-speed transmissions for 1967-68 were supplied by Muncie (left); 1969 was Hurst. Names appear on the shift levers.

Camaro insignia is placed above door-pull.

A combination door-pull and arm rest is provided.

This crank operates the window; vent is rotated open by hand.

Door handle is located just ahead of arm rest.

1967 Standard Interior door panel.

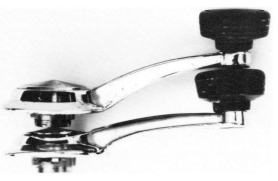

Both Standard and Custom inside door lock knobs match interior colors.

Rear window cranks have more curve than front, but otherwise interchange; Standard & Custom interiors.

Door release is recessed into molded arm rest on Custom Interior door panel.

Floor carpeting is applied at bottom of door panel for added effect.

1967 Custom Interior door panel.

1967 standard Strato-Bucket front seat.

Front seat backs are mechanically latched. Release is by chromed knob on lower seat back.

Chromed knob at side of seat operates latch for fore-and-aft adjustment.

1967 Custom Interior Strato-Bucket front seat.

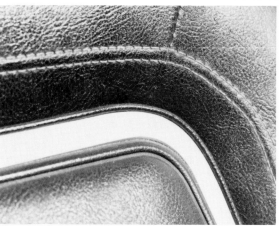

Custom Interior seats have white or black contrasting insert stripes. A combination of sewn and heat-stiched seams appears.

Ash trays, built into rear arm rests, are a feature of all Convertibles and Custom Interior Sport Coupes.

1967 standard Convertible rear seat.

A folding Rear Seat option permits seat to be tilted forward for added carrying capacity.

The Custom Interior provides dual lamps on the rear quarters in place of the standard single dome light.

1967 Cusom Interior Sport Coupe rear seat.

1967

Available only in the Sport Coupe model, a Strato-Back front seat was offered as an Option. With folding arm rest raised, the seat provided reasonable three abreast seating. Its design, however, prevents use of center console.

The standard heater controls appear in a panel placed at the top center of the instrument panel. Optional air-conditioning called for the replacement of this panel with appropriate controls and a center air outlet (above left).

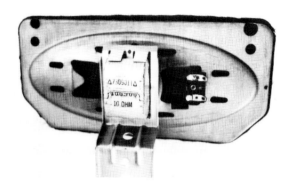

Radio offerings for 1967 are monaural. Speaker is located under top surface of instrument panel and is held in place by integral bracket. An optional rear seat speaker was also offered.

The AM pushbutton radio (left) was offered either with single speaker or with an additional optional rear seat speaker as was the alternate option, an AM-FM monaural radio (above). Antennas furnished with these Options were right-front fender mounted, but yet another Option provided a rear-mounted antenna.

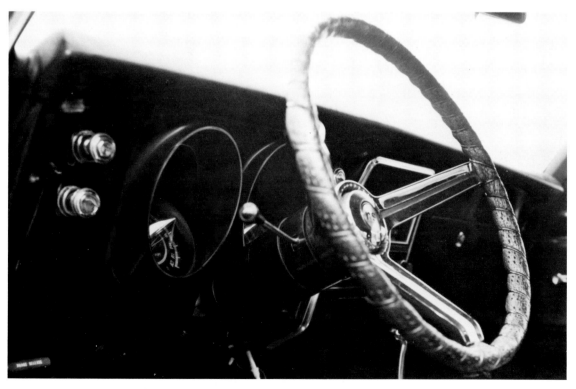

1967 Instrument panel. Steering wheel wrap is aftermarket accessory.

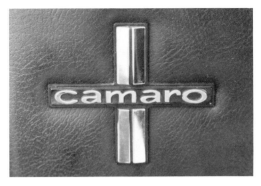

Camaro insignia is placed on the glove box door at right of instrument panel.

A glove compartment light, included with Custom Interior, but optionally separately available, is controlled by closing the door against this push button.

Tire pressure information is contained on a decal applied to the inside of the glove box door.

Front and rear seat belts are both standard.

Standard front seat belt retractors are placed outboard of the front seats.

View of rear of instrument cluster shows unique flexible printed circuit wiring.

Gauge cluster assembly contains speedometer (left) and *either* fuel gauge or tachometer.

Fuel gauge instrument also contains panels at bottom which light appropriately to display GEN, right turn arrow, TEMP functions.

Standard 120 mph speedometer also contains display windows for OIL, left turn arrow, and BRAKE functions. When Special Instrumentation option (page 77) is ordered, OIL is replaced by low FUEL display.

1967 instruments have white letters printed on black background.

Deeply convex clear plastic protective lenses are used to protect the speedometer and matching fuel or tachometer gauges.

75

1967

6000 red line; 7000 maximum. Used with 396 cu in engine, mechanical lifter version.

5000 red line; 7000 maximum. Used with small block engine.

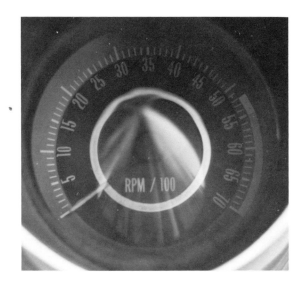

5500 red line; 7000 maximum. Used with big block hydraulic lifter versions.

Accessory Speed Warning speedometer adds an audible signal at preset speed and re-places original speedometer.

Accessory electirc clock can be mounted on in-strument panel or console.

Interchangeable inserts adjust for Powerglide (upper right), Turbo Hydra-Matic (right) or 3- or 4-speed (above).

Available only on V-8 cars, and only together with console, Optional Special Instrumentation package also includes tachometer on panel.

Tab helps in opening storage compartment in console.

Seat belt latch can be secured to this tab when not in use.

An ash tray, easily accessible to rear seat passengers is provided at back of console. Beneath is illuminated courtesy light.

Optional rear window defroster, available in the Sport Coupe only, directs air over rear window. It mounts beneath rear package shelf behind suitable screen.

The Delco stereo tape deck with four speakers is available as a factory-installed Option in place of a radio (unless air conditioning is ordered). It is also available as a Dealer-installed Custom Accessory, and is often then mounted on the lid of a console.

When accessory stereo tape player is console-mounted, it's controls are placed facing forward; shown here on a 1969 console, the unit can be adjusted by sound only.

1967 Convertible with Custom Interior

1968 Camaro
the "hugger" from Chevrolet

1968 exterior colors are:

A Tuxedo Black	R Matador Red	N Cordovan Maroon
L Teal Blue	F Island Teal	H Grecian Green
G Ash Gold	U Sequoia Green	Y Butternut Yellow
D Grotto Blue	P Seafrost Green	E Fathom Blue
T Palomino Ivory	C Ermine White	K Tripoli Turquoise

For 1968, the Camaro was virtually a 1967 carryover. Minor modifications were made in some appearance items, for example, the parking lights, grille center emblem, front header nameplate, etc., were all revised. More Options were made available, and several safety-related items were added as standard (break-away ash tray, windshield pillar padding, non-glare (dull chrome) steering wheel trim, hazard warning knob, rear-view mirror back and mounting bracket), side marker lamps, etc.

The most obvious change was the incorporation of "Astro Ventilation", a flow-through air system which eliminated the vent windows used in 1967. At the rear, shock absorbers are stagger-mounted (ahead and behind the rear axle) and a new multi-leaf spring incorporated to reduce wheel hop.

Exhaust emission controls are incorporated on all engines, Positive Crankcase Ventilation (PCV) being only one of the controls. The other is either a Controlled Combustion System (CCS) or the Air Injector System (AIR) with the AIR used on the manual transmission and 396 hydraulic lifter engines and the CCS on all others.

1968 CAMARO POWER TEAMS

Engines Bore & Stroke	Equipment Compression Ratio	Transmission	Rear Axle Ratio Without Air Conditioning*				Rear Axle Ratio With Air Conditioning		
			Std.	Econ.	Perform.	Spec.	Std.	Econ.	Perform.
Standard Engines									
140-hp Turbo-Thrift 230 Six 3.875 x 3.25	1-Bbl. Carb. Hyd. Lifters 8.5:1	3-Speed (2.85:1 Low)	3.08:1	2.73:1	3.55:1		3.08:1		3.55:1
		4-Speed (2.85:1 Low)	3.08:1	2.73:1	3.55:1		3.08:1		3.55:1
		Powerglide	2.73:1‡	2.56:1	3.55:1		3.08:1		3.55:1
210-hp Turbo-Fire 327 V8 4.00 x 3.25	2-Bbl. Carb. Hyd. Lifters 8.75:1	3-Speed (2.54:1 Low)	3.08:1	2.73:1	3.55:1		3.08:1		3.55:1
		4-Speed (2.54:1 Low)	3.08:1	2.73:1	3.55:1		3.08:1		3.55:1
		Powerglide	2.73:1‡	2.56:1	3.55:1		3.08:1		3.55:1
Extra-Cost Engines									
155-hp Turbo-Thrift 250 Six 3.875 x 3.53	1-Bbl. Carb. Hyd. Lifters 8.5:1	3-Speed (2.85:1 Low)	3.08:1	2.73:1	3.55:1		3.08:1		3.55:1
		4-Speed (2.85:1 Low)	3.08:1	2.73:1	3.55:1		3.08:1		3.55:1
		Powerglide	2.73:1‡	2.56:1	3.55:1		3.08:1		3.55:1
275-hp Turbo-Fire 327 V8 4.00 x 3.25	4-Bbl. Carb. Hyd. Lifters 10.0:1	3-Speed (2.54:1 Low)	3.08:1	2.73:1	3.55:1		3.08:1		3.55:1
		4-Speed (2.54:1 Low)	3.07:1	2.73:1	3.55:1		3.07:1		3.55:1
		Powerglide	2.73:1‡	2.56:1	3.55:1		3.08:1		3.55:1
295-hp Turbo-Fire 350 V8 4.00 x 3.48	4-Bbl. Carb. Hyd. Lifters 10.25:1	3-Speed (2.54:1 Low)	3.31:1	3.07:1	3.55:1		3.31:1	3.07:1	3.55:1
		Sp. 3-Speed (2.41:1 Low)	3.31:1	3.07:1	3.55:1	3.73:1	3.31:1	3.07:1	3.55:1
		4-Speed (2.52:1 Low)				3.73:1 4.10:1 4.56:1 4.88:1			
		Powerglide	3.07:1	2.73:1	3.31:1	3.55:1 3.73:1	3.07:1	2.73:1	3.31:1
325-hp Turbo-Jet 396 V8 4.094 x 3.76	4-Bbl. Carb. Hyd. Lifters 10.25:1	Sp. 3-Speed (2.41:1 Low)	3.07:1	2.73:1	3.31:1		3.07:1	2.73:1	3.31:1
		4-Speed (2.52:1 Low)	3.07:1	2.73:1	3.31:1		3.07:1	2.73:1	3.31:1
		Turbo Hydra-Matic	2.73:1†	2.56:1	3.07:1		2.73:1‡		3.07:1

*Positraction required for 4.10:1, 4.56:1, 4.88:1, optional for all other ratios. †3.07:1 when Rally Sport is specified. ‡3.08:1 when Rally Sport is specified.

Again in 1968, Dealers were provided with a host of accessories with which the new cars could be customized at the buyers option. Among these were:

Air conditioning
Stereo tape players
AM-FM radio
Stereo multiplex unit
AM radio
Rear seat speaker
Fire extinguisher
Litter container
Highway emergency kit
Ventilated seat cushions
Auto compass
Hand portable spotlight
Rear seat belt retractors
Ski rack
Rear deck lid luggage carrier
Front & rear bumper guards
Door edge guards
Wheel covers (4 types)
GM Vigilante fiber option light monitoring system
Locking gas cap
Tri-volume horn
Spare tire lock
Right-hand rear view mirror
Temperature-controlled fan
Rubber floor mats
Tachometer
Rear window defroster
Power brakes
Cruise-Master speed control
Electric clock
Vanity Visor mirror
Glove compartment light
Underhood light
Tissue dispenser
Ash tray light
Luggage compartment light
Courtesy lights

custom feature accessories for 1968 CAMARO

You wouldn't expect anything to match Corvette's sports car ride and handling.

Bucket seats behind a long, low hood. Bump-smoothing, curve-straightening four-wheel independent suspension. V8s that range from a standard 327 cubic inches up to a 427 that you can order. New full door-glass styling. New Astro Ventilation. More beauty, more excitement than ever. And *still* America's only true production sports car.

Seeking to extend its image as a sports car, Camaro advertisements sought the benefit of association with the readily-accepted Corvette.

But when you drive "The Hugger"... will you be surprised!

Bucket seats behind a long, low hood. A smooth-riding, road-hugging improved suspension system. V8s you can order that start at 327 cubic inches and work their way up to 396. Sleek full door-glass styling, like Corvette. Flow-through Astro Ventilation, like Corvette. Command drive a Camaro . . . Corvette's road-hugging running mate!

Camaro '68 Corvette

Be smart! Be sure! Buy now at your Chevrolet dealer's.

1968 Camaro Sport Coupe

A change in identification emblem reverses position of words but maintains style similarity with 1967 badges (compare page 35). Emblem is now one-piece item.

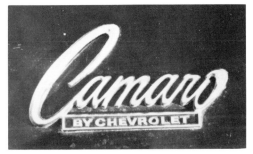

Mr. Kent Parnell, Oceanside, California

A new emblem also appears for 1968, and horizontal grille bars are painted satin-silver for wider effect.

Restyled front end displays rectangular parking lamps in place of round ones of 1967 (page 36).

Bright metal trim emphasises appearance of headlamps.

Parking lamps remain ON when headlamps are turned ON, a new safety feature for 1968.

Front header panel stripe was available as a customizing option with either 350 or 396 engines.

Hood is secured by pin and sliding latch.

Full-width front window is unchanged.

Script CAMARO on fender flanks replaces the 1967 block letters (page 39).

Basic hood is unchanged from 1967.

Front marker light.

New for 1968 are side marker lights on front and rear fenders.

Lower body trim strip is unchanged.

1968 SPORT COUPE

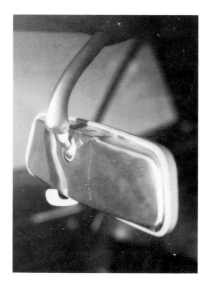

A 1968 safety-related feature is the new rear view mirror with its deflecting ball-joint suspended mount.

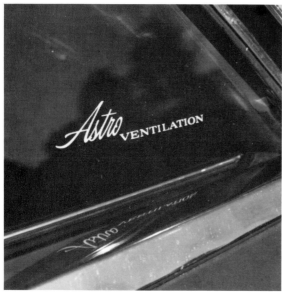

Astro Ventilation, new for 1968, is a controlled air flow system with outside air admitted through vent-ports on the instrument panel and exiting through the lower rear rocker panels. Decal appears on side windows.

Vent windows are eliminated for 1968 with the introduction of Astro Ventilation.

Eliminated ventipanes are a primary 1968 visual identification aid.

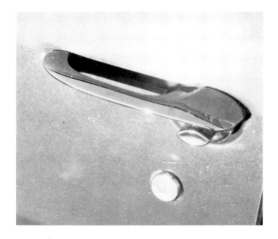

Pushbutton outside door handles are unchanged; door edge guards are accessories.

Rear quarter windows are unchanged.

Doors appear wider with elimination of vent windows but are actually unchanged.

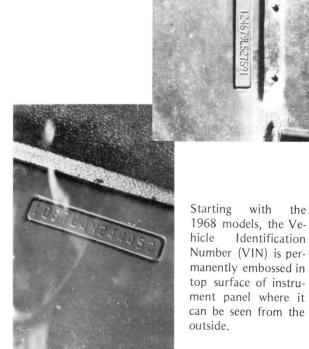

Starting with the 1968 models, the Vehicle Identification Number (VIN) is permanently embossed in top surface of instrument panel where it can be seen from the outside.

89

Appearance of rear quarter is changed with the addition of side marker lights, a safety-oriented government requirement on all cars for 1968.

Side marker lens bears Guide name and model year, a GM continuing practice. Unlike front lens which is amber, the rear lens is red.

New one-piece Camaro emblem appears also on rear deck lid.

Rear quarter view greatly resembles that of 1967 Sport Coupe (page 42), but side marker light easily identifies the 1968 model.

As in 1967, the fuel filler cap is a twist-on type, painted to match body color unless RS or SS options apply.

Fuel filler cap, unlike RS and SS types is not leashed to the body (page 63).

Although resembling the 1967 tail lights, the 1968 style does differ. In 1967 (page 43), the red portion is longer than the white back up lens; the 1968 lenses are about equal in length.

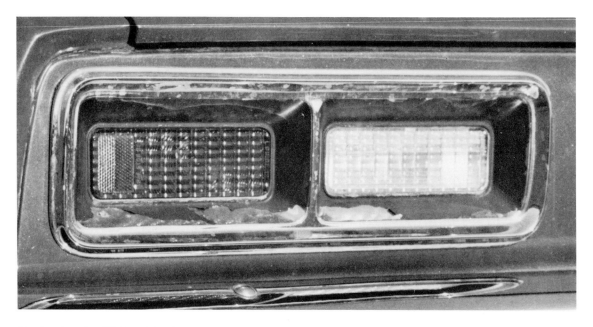

Black-painted taillight highlighting is a 1968 feature, along with a more pronounced divider between the two lenses.

On cars equipped with Positraction, a decal is placed on the underside of rear deck lid cautioning hazard involved in jacking the car.

All models are provided with a decal advising jacking instructions and spare wheel storage instructions.

The basic Sport Coupe could, again in 1968, be upgraded by ordering the Rally Sport Option. This included the concealed headlights with parking and directional lights below the bumper, RS emblem on the grill, back-up lights below the rear bumper, RS emblem on fuel filler cap, lower body side molding, wheel opening moldings, "rally-sport" on fenders, etc.

1968 Camaro Rally Sport

Mr. Andrew Bomis, San Diego, California

Obvious identification feature of the Rally Sport is its concealed headlights.

Operated by electric motors in 1967, the revised 1968 system now uses vacuum-operated solenoids to open headlamp doors.

RS grille emblem is used in place of standard grille ornament (page 86).

A painted lamp housing is used in 1968 in place of the chromed item employed in 1967 (page 50).

RS Taillight has single red lens and places back up light below bumper.

Appearance of rear view is changed by solid red rear lamp as compared to standard red/white (page 92).

RS fuel filler cap is unchanged from 1967.

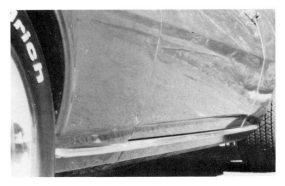

Standard 1968 Camaro shown for comparison.

Uniquely shaped RS lower body trim strip emphasises apparent narrowed body section.

Wheel opening lip moldings are included in Rally Sport option, but are also available separately.

1968 CAMARO SS

Featuring a special hood with decorative louvres, (stack-type on the 396 cu in engine), SS grille emblem, underhood insulation, special suspension items, front header panel stripe, red (or white) stripe tires, SS identification on front fender and fuel filler cap, the SS option was available either singly or in conjunction with the RS features as shown here. The special SS350 identifications (page 57) used on 1967 models has been discontinued and the grille emblem now simply reads SS.

1968 Camaro SS with Rally Sport option

Mr. C.F. Nichols, Oceanside, California

RS option, also included on this Camaro SS includes the hide-away headlights, but SS grille emblem takes precedence over the RS insignia.

Header panel stripe, a feature of the SS option, highlights conventional 1968 Camaro emblem.

Full width bumper protects front fender corners.

The SS option incorporates the "louvered" hood first used in 1967 as standard, but the same option with the 396 cu in engine calls for a special hood (page 108).

Engine size is specified by appropriate front fender emblem.

Astro Ventilation, introduced on the 1968 model, brings with it an exhaust vent placed on the rear door jamb (above right) which circulates air down behind the rocker panels.

Bright roof drip molding and belt line molding (also visible in photo below) is part of the Rally Sport option, but could also be ordered separately.

Chromed push-button door handles are unchanged.

Optional bright metal belt line molding extends to back of rear quarter window.

1968 SS insignia is a one-piece emblem.

One-piece insignia is affixed to fender flanks beneath the standard Camaro script.

Dual red taillight of the RS option is actually a single lens, not two.

GM's practice of identifying lenses with model year is continued with applicable "68" shown here.

SS fuel filler cap is unique to that Option.

Rectangular back up lights are placed below the bumper with the RS option.

Identical to RS option (with which this car is also equipped), the SS rear end is distinctive only at the fuel filler cap.

Rear package shelf (called "foundation" by Chevrolet) of Sport Coupe is convenient place to mount optional defogger or stereo speakers.

Bright metal trim of rear window is standard Camaro feature.

1968 CAMARO SS

The SS option when ordered together with the 325 horse-power 396 cu. in. Turbo-Jet engine had all of the same features as mentioned previously on page 98. In addition, there was a black-painted rear panel, and a new hood (page 108) used in 1968 exclusively with this engine.

1968 Camaro SS

Mr. Ed Boortz, El Cajon, California

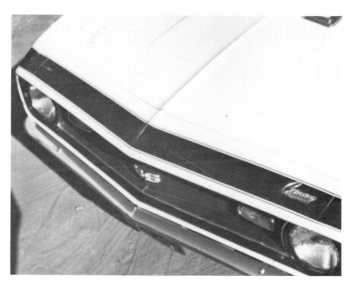

Grille of standard Camaro exhibits sharper angle than flatter Rally Sport concealed headlight grille.

To accommodate sharp angle of standard grille, SS (or RS) emblem has sharper bend when viewed from above.

Although similar in appearance to standard version, SS emblem to be used on concealed headlight grille is flatter.

Engine identification appears on fenders in place of SS insignia used in 1967 (page 57).

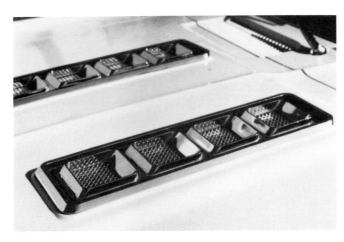

Dual "stack-type" hood escutcheons are visible evidence of
the 396 cu. in. engines.

Although appearance is of working ports, hood emblems are actually non-functional; dress-up only.

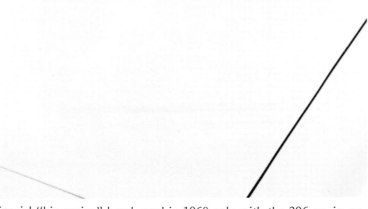

Special "big engine" hood, used in 1968 only with the 396 cu. in. engine option. Other engines were provided with "louvred" hood (page
101).

In addition to standard Camaro script, the special SS emblem appears on the fender flanks in place of engine identification used in 1967 (page 59).

Rear panel is flat-black painted on the Camaro SS with the 396 cu. in. engine option. This is the only model on which this is done.

Special fuel filler cap is part of SS option.

Black-painted area around lights is standard for 1968, painting of the panel itself is limited as above.

Following practice, SS emblem is placed at hub, even with optional Deluxe steering wheel.

Optional Deluxe steering wheel has two horn-blowing pushbuttons in the horizontal spokes.

1968 CAMARO CONVERTIBLE

The 1968 Camaro Convertible was the second year of only three years of manufacture of this body style. With a soft waterproofed canvas top and rolled-up windows, it was relatively quiet and exceptionally comfortable. With its top folded and its windows lowered it became an exhilarating way to travel.

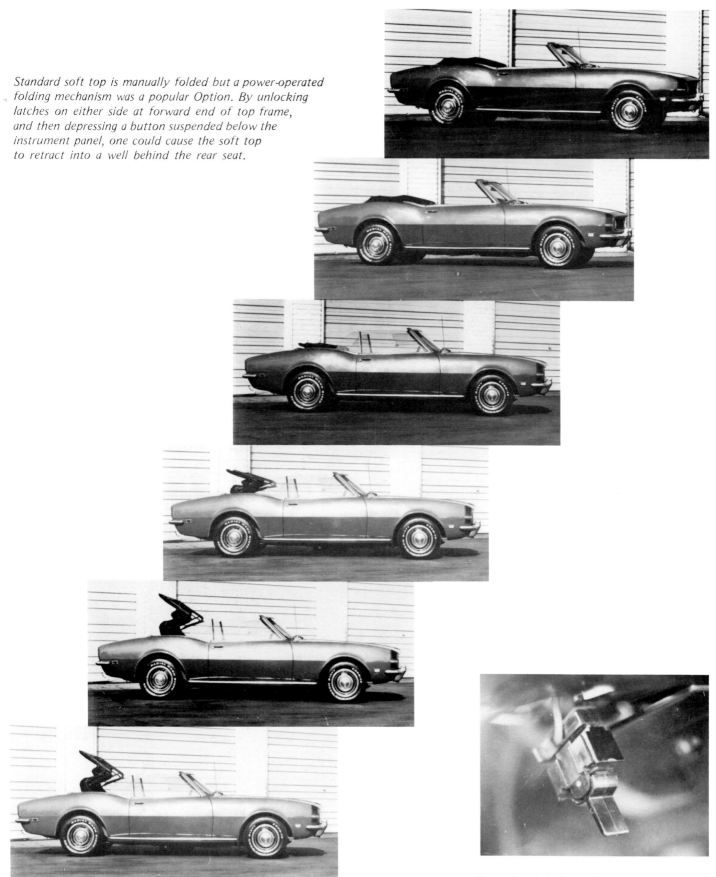

Standard soft top is manually folded but a power-operated folding mechanism was a popular Option. By unlocking latches on either side at forward end of top frame, and then depressing a button suspended below the instrument panel, one could cause the soft top to retract into a well behind the rear seat.

Control switch for optional power operated folding top is suspended beneath instrument panel.

The attractive Convertible was the second of two basic body styles offered for 1968. Already nearing the end of its production life, only 20,440 units of this desirable model were produced.

1968 Camaro Convertible

Mr. Dan Smith, Leucadia, California

Convertible top is offered in black, white, or blue. Note bright metal trim on windshield post unlike painted metal on Sport Coupe (page 101).

Convertible interior is available only in all-vinyl trim unlike the Sport Coupe which also offers houndstooth fabric-and-black-vinyl as an Option.

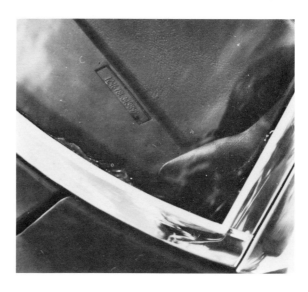

Vehicle Identification Number again appears permanently embossed into the instrument panel.

1968 CAMARO Z28

1968 Z28 Camaro folder is one of few literature items available for the model.

On November 26, 1966, only weeks after the public introduction of the new Camaro, Chevrolet unveiled its answer to Ford's High Performance Mustang at Riverside Raceway in California. A new Option (RPO Z28), unlisted in the 1967 Sales Folders, provided muscle, performance and more.

The Option featured a new engine, a 302 cubic inch version, facetiously rated at only 290 horsepower. Developed to meet a racing class requirement that limited volume to 305 cubic inches, this engine was a clever evolution that incorporated the existing 327 cubic inch block and the crankshaft of the existing 283 engine giving an effective volume of 302.5 cubic inches! Other items included mechanical lifters for high revolution capability, and a new "tuned inlet" manifold, matching both the volume of Ford's engine and its intake system.

The first "production" models, some 25 units, were produced by the end of the second week of Janaury of 1967, but in all, only 602 were produced in all of 1967.

Other than its distinct stripe pattern, initially there was no special identification, but early on, 302 emblems made their appearance on the front fenders and carried through the early 1968 models. A running change in 1968 brought the familair Z28 emblems to the front fender (page 204).

An unusual feature of the Z28 was the optional plenum air intake (RPO Z28C) which provided a duct assembly from the plenum chamber below the windshield and a new air cleaner; air entering the grill ahead of the windshield was thus ducted directly to the carburetor under some relative pressure. Together with exhaust headers and a transistorized ignition system, these three items were options shipped " in the trunk" for installation by the Dealers.

Distinctive stripes became a delete option in 1968.

1968 Camaro Sport Coupe with Z28 Option   *Mr. Greg Mullendore, San Diego, California*

302 emblem was used on front fenders of early 1968 production; later in year, the familiar Z28 embelm appeared.

CAMARO WITH SPECIAL HIGH PERFORMANCE OPTION Z28
        . . . as announced in December 1966

Body
    Standard Camaro (Sport Coupe only) with special paint stripes and (coming) 302 emblems.
Steering
    Power steering same; manual steering ratio 24:1, 20:1 available (standard is 28.3:1).
Front & Rear Suspensions
    Heavy duty springs and shock absorbers, rear axle radius rod provided to reduce power hop. 3.73 rear axle standard for Z28 with 3.07 and 3.55 ratios available.
Brakes
    Front power disc brakes; rear standard drum brakes. Heavy duty brake linings option available.
Engine
    New 302 cu. in. mechanical lifter high performance engine. Chromed rocker covers, filler cap, vent cap, and air cleaner cover. The 302 engine is same as the 327 cu. in. except for crankshaft, pistons, camshaft, oil pump, oil pan baffling, mechanical lifters, and tuned runner inlet manifold. Carburetor is an 800 CMF Holley with 3/8" fuel lines. Open element air cleaner; Distributor same as 350 cu. in. engine item; five blade fan assembly with 2300-2600 RPM operating speed capability.
Transmission
    Muncie 4-speed close ratio standard; alternate gear ratios available with option axle.
Exhaust
    Dual exhaust pipes and low tone mufflers without resonators.
Wheels & Tires
    New steel 15 x 6 wheel with trim ring and hub cap same as Chevrolet disc brake option. Tire is nylon 7.35 x 15 red stripe high performance type.

1968 Camaro Sport Coupe with Z28 Option   *Mr. Ray Miller, Oceanside, California*

Unique contrasting hood stripes are mark of the Z28.

Z28 was equipped with new steel 15 x 6 wheels. Trim ring and hub caps are standard.

Stripes extend over the cowl intake grilles.

Standard tires for the 1967 Z28 are nylon red stripe 7.35 x 15. 1968 size is E70 x 15.

New 302 engine insignia is used on front fenders in early 1968; later had Z28 emblem.

Standard rear wheel brakes are drum type. Optional heavy duty metallic linings were offered. Few cars had a 4-wheel disc brake option offered late in 1968.

The tire pressure decal located on glove box door refers to the special 15 inch wheels and differs from decal on other models.

The unique Z28 contrasting stripe pattern is continued on the rear deck. New optional rear spoiler is painted to match.

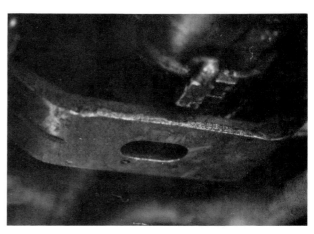

Standard heavy cross member supports rear of transmission.

Standard exhaust manifolds were optionally replaced by tube headers on Z28. When ordered, they were delivered to the Dealer for installation, not factory-installed.

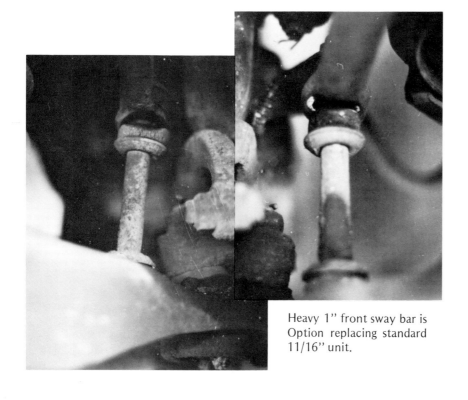

Heavy 1" front sway bar is Option replacing standard 11/16" unit.

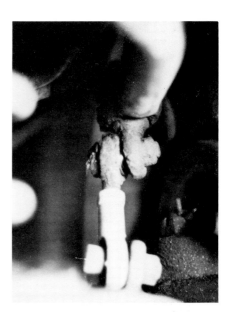

Many low-production, specialty, race-oriented items were available; among them an *adjustable* front sway bar for cornering control.

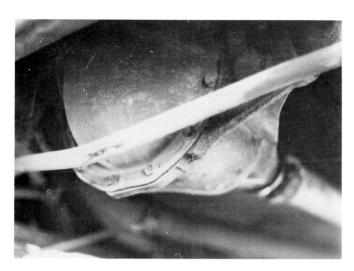

Not part of original Z28 package, an accessory 7/8" rear sway bar has been added. This assembly subsequently became standard on the 1970 Z28. Differential housing is "12 bolt" type, Positration a recommended available Option.

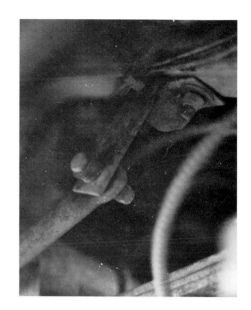

Accessory rear sway bar is secured to the body stringers.

In 1967, a traction bar was added to prevent rear axle "hop" on acceleration, a problem emphasised by Camaro's standard single-leaf rear spring. The Z28 corrected this problem by staggering rear shock absorbers and incorporating multi-leafed springs.

Multi-leaf rear springs replaced standard "monoplate" spring.

Exhaust exits behind rear wheel.

Air cleaner is an open-element, chrome cover assembly. Appropriate decal is standard.

Radiator inlet and outlet hoses are standard as used with 327 engine.

Chromed oil filler cap, vent cap, and rocker covers are standard for 1968 Z28.

Power-assisted front disc brakes, standard on Z28, are operated by under-hood unit.

Carburetor is Holly 780 CFM 4-V using 3/8" fuel lines.

Z28 water inlet allows for insertion of temperature probe as alternate to unit in block.

Casting information identifies manifold.

Aluminum "tuned runner" high rise manifold is unique to Z28 302 cu. in. engine.

Camaro emblem appears above arm rest.

STANDARD INTERIOR

Standard interior door panel has bolt-on arm rest which serves as a door-pull.

Inside door latch handle extends forward through arm rest housing.

Window crank knobs are same on Standard and Custom interior panels.

Inside door lock knobs, on both Standard and Custom interiors match color of upholstery.

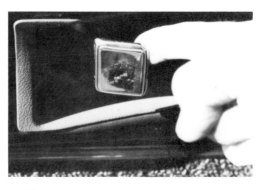

Inside door latch release rotates outward from door.

Similar Camaro script appears on door panel.

Upper handle is Standard type; Custom Interior handle below.

CUSTOM INTERIOR

Custom Interior door panel features molded arm rest and recessed door latch release handle.

Window crank knobs match interior color.

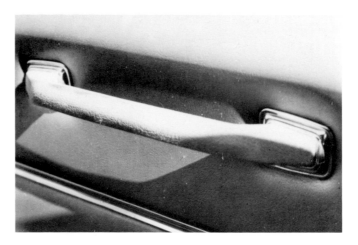

Separate door pull is feature of Custom Interior only.

Standard Interior rear seat of 1968 Convertible features arm rests and ash trays.

Standard interior of Sport Coupe lacks ash trays and arm rests, but these *are* included with Custom Interior.

1968 Sport Coupe front seat area; Standard interior.

1968 STANDARD INTERIOR

1968 Standard interior seats are same as 1967. Upholstery is vinyl only.

Back of seats, soft vinyl in 1967, are hard, formed plastic for 1968.

All front seat backs are latched, with release knob at lower seat back.

Custom Interior seats feature more attractive pattern. Not shown is alternate optional vinyl-and-houndstooth cloth upholstery.

1968 CUSTOM INTERIOR

Bright metal unique insignia is featured on Custom Interior seat backs.

The fold-down rear seat, offered again in 1968, provides an additional luggage-carrying area behind the front seats. Shown here in a 1968 Custom Interior Sport Coupe, it is an unobtrusive option in its normal seating position, differing little from the conventional rear seat. However, lowering the seat back exposes a neatly carpeted package tray.

New for 1968, a latch is provided to lock seat back in upright position. Cushion is shaped to clear.

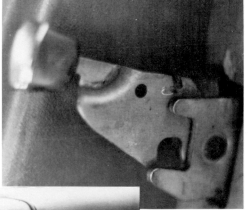

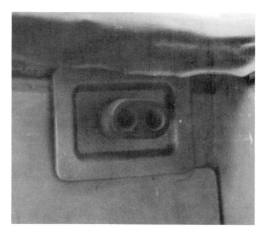

Rubber bumper on left side of car prevents rattles.

Back of folded rear seat cushion is nicely carpeted to serve as package-carrying shelf.

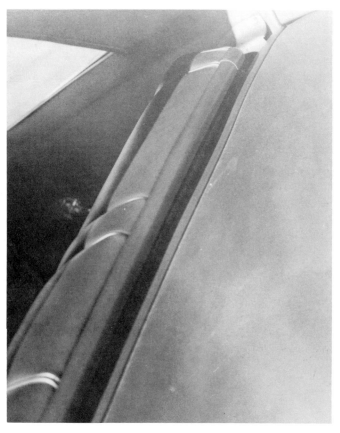

A metal seat-back rail is evidence of optional folding seat (Compare page 78).

Optional Sport Styled steering wheel is also used on other Chevrolets including Corvette.

Incoming air outlets are at ends of instrument panel. Each can be rotated or blocked independently.

Horn button is at hub of the wheel.

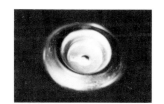

Glove compartment is provided with push-button locking latch.

Wood grain accents are part of Special Interior dress up Option.

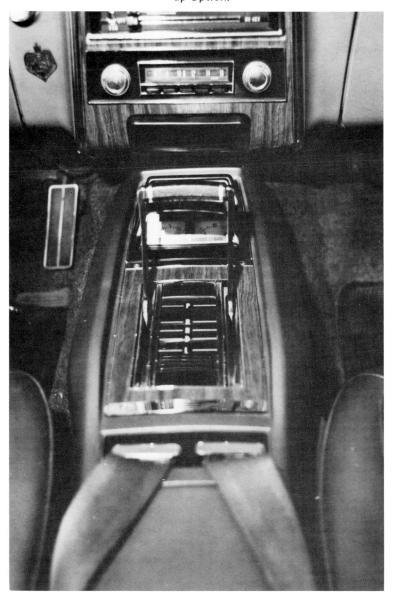

Ignition switch remains on instrument panel.

The new console for 1968 provides recessed tabs for securing seat belts.

Standard 3-spoke steering wheel resembles 1967 part.

Camaro horn button appears at center of standard steering wheel.

Appropriately labeled horn buttons interchange depending upon the Option selected.

Part of the claimed safety-related improvements for 1968 was the replacement of formerly brightly polished control levers with a dull "Non-glare" brushed finish. These included the steering wheel spokes and horn button.

Identification escutcheons, metal in 1967, are replaced in 1968 with plastic parts.

1968 instruments have black letters against silver background. Speedometer displays to 120 MPH, and in addition to direction signal, OIL and BRAKE.

Matching fuel guage also has direction signal arrow and indicator lights to read GEN and TEMP.

These instruments, part of Special Instrumentation Group which also includes tachometer, replace lights with instruments displaying Temperature, Oil Pressure, Ammeter, and Fuel level. With this Option comes a FUEL insert in the speedometer replacing OIL, and displaying a low fuel level warning.

Special Instrumentation Option is mounted on forward end of the associated required console, with instrument faces angled back to provide better visibility.

Optional Four-Season factory air conditioning provides behind-the-instrument-panel installation complete with added center vent above a special control panel.

The standard heater control panel interchanges but lettering differs.

Radio antenna normally mounts on right front fender; an extra-cost added option permits rear mounting.

Optional five-pushbutton AM radio. Just below is ash tray, standard on all models.

Front seat belts are firmly anchored to the drive shaft tunnel.

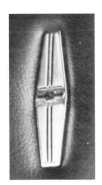

Custom Interior seats display unique insert used only in 1968.

GM's Fisher Body Division built the Camaro bodies; their trademark appears on door sill plates.

Standard seat belt buckle bears GM mark.

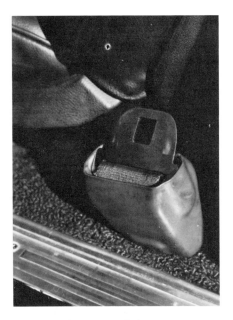

Standard front seat belt retractors are furnished at sides of seats.

Releasing this latch permits front seat fore-and-aft adjustment.

1968

New for 1968 is a stirrup-like shifter for the floor-mounted automatic transmissions.

Powerglide automatic transmission's shift pattern is P-R-N-D-L.

Turbo Hydra-Matic transmission (used only with the big 396 cu. in. engine) has a P-R-N-3-2-1 shift pattern.

Metal trim plates on the foot pedals and accelerator are part of the Special Interior Group.

Incorporation of the optional Disc Brakes is indicated by a labeled disc on the foot pedal.

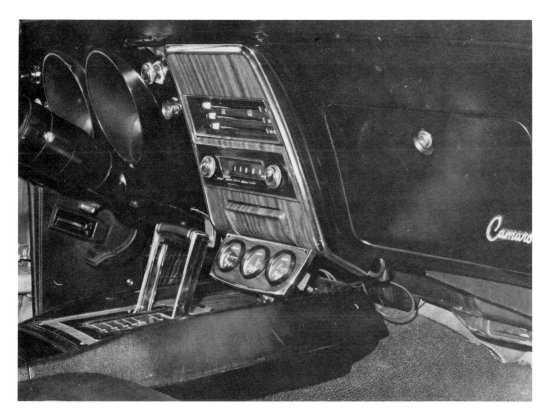

After-market accessory gauges shown here are often owner-installed in place of correct factory option gauge assembly (page 133).

Column-mounted transmission shifters are standard; floor mounted location is an Option which includes the Console when ordered for automatic transmissions. Three-speed manual shifters are optionally available as floor-mounts *without the console* on six cylinder engines and 327 cu. in. V8 only.

Foot-operated parking brake is standard.

Hazard warning (four-way flasher) switch knob continues to be found on the steering column.

New console (page 214) fits nicely between front seats.

Located at rear end of console is an ash tray, and below it, a courtesy light operated by switches in the door jambs.

Standard 3-speed shift pattern console plate.

1968 (left) and 1969 4-speed shift pattern console plates.

Rear view of 1968 & 1969 plates show difference in construction. Sliding blocking plate is eliminated in 1969, otherwise interchangeable.

The Camaro dual-carburetor manifold known as the "Cross Ram Unit" was the ultimate performance option and was intended for the Z28 (although it would, of course, fit any 327 engine). It featured two Holly 600 cfm carburetors mounted on a two-piece aluminum manifold and claimed an added 50-60 HP to the already potent 302 engines. An estimated 600 units were built, about 125 in 1968, the balance in 1969 and all were sold over the Dealers' counters, not factory installed.

1968-69 Camaro Cross Ram manifold is formed of two aluminum castings (right and below) forming two plenum chambers each feeding four separate cylinders.

Although single-pumper Hollys were used in 1968, by 1969 dual double-pumper carburetors were substituted to end fuel starvation problems.

1968 air cleaner employed oval base, air filter, and chromed cover.

The 1968 air cleaner (left) was continued in 1969, and this style was offered as well. It was foam rubber sealed to an accessory fiber-glass accessory hood.

The unique 1968 "Tik-Tok-Tach" is a tachometer and clock combined into one instrument and furnished as part of the Special Instrumentation Group along with the console-mounted instruments shown on page 133.

5000 Red Line, 7000 max, 350 & 396 cu. in. V8 with hydraulic lifters.

5500 Red Line, 7000 max used with 327 cu. in. V8.

6000 Red Line, 7000 max 302 and 396 cu. in. with mechanical lifters.

The Speed Warning Indicator is a similar speedometer with an adjustable pointer which is pre-set to the desired maximum speed. When reached, it causes a warning buzzer to sound thus alerting the driver to slow down. It became available in 1967 and, with suitable speedometer face modification, remained available in 1968 and 1969.

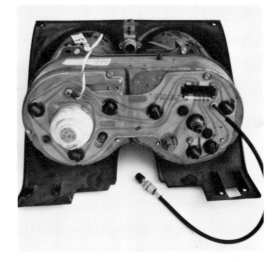

Back of 1968 Speedwarning instrument cluster also showing installed tachometer. Note larger hole in printed circuit to accommodate tachometer hub (standard p/c shown on page 75).

Bright belt line molding and roof rain gutter are part of dress up Style Trim Group, available separately, but also included as part of the Rally Sport Option.

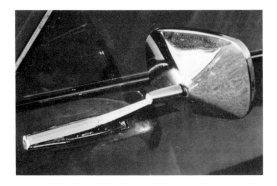

New rectangular mirror replaces the round one used in 1967.

Door edge guards are a separately available Option, but are also included with front and rear floor mats, deluxe seat belts, and front and rear bumper guards as the Appearance Guard Group option.

An Option introduced in 1967, was the Comfortilt Steering Wheel which offered an adjustment of the steering wheel angle and remained popular through the entire period. It was available only with floor-mounted transmission shifters, not with standard column-mounted units.

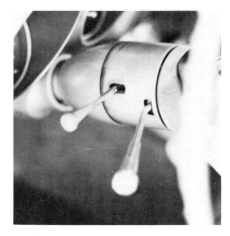

Adjustment is made by depressing lever beneath turn signal arm to release safety latch.

Wheel can be adjusted through large angle from near-vertical to almost 40 degrees.

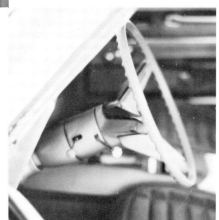

Power operated windows also were available starting with the 1967 model. The master control switch, mounted on the left side door panel, operates both side and the quarter windows. A single-switch control is mounted at each of the other three windows.

A console-mounted electric clock Option was available as an alternate to the more elaborate Special Instrumentation Group.

Front and rear bumper guards were an available Option separately, and also as a part of the Special Appearance Guard Group along with door edge guards, floor mats, and deluxe seat belts.

Although each item was available for purchase separately, the use of front and rear spoilers in 1968 was essentially limited to their appearance on the Z28.

Stereo radio or tape rear speakers were mounted under the rear package shelf of the Sport Coupe; on back of rear seat of the Convertible.

Head "restraint" can be raised for comfort.

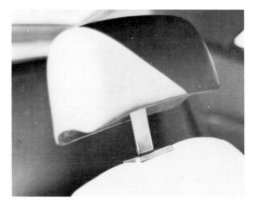

These chromed plates are used as escutcheons on top of seats when head rests are installed.

In advance of upcoming government requirements for them, Head "Restraints" were offered as Options in 1967 and 1968. These were adjustable cushions applied on driver's and front passenger's seats only.

1969 CAMARO
Putting you first, keeps us first

146

1969 saw changes in the Camaro which, while significant, are not always obvious. As an example, an increase of approximately one half inch in the tread width improved handling and also appearance. Cosmetic changes included an optional simulated rear fender louver and available two-tone exteriors. Added available options made the car even more tractable, and Camaro's selection, for the second time in only three years, as Indianapolis Speedway's Pace Car raised interest to even greater heights.

Exterior Colors for 1969:

50 Dover White	55 Azure Turquoise
53 Glacier Blue	59 Frost Green
51 Dusk Blue (dark)	67 Burgandy
71 LeMans Blue (bright)	69 Cortez Silver
65 Olympic Gold	52 Garnet Red
61 Burnished Brown	57 Fathom Green (dark)
79 Rallye Green (bright)	72 Hugger Orange (bright)
	76 Dayona Yellow (bright)

Also, for the first time, two tone combinations as follows:
53 Glacier Blue (lower)/Dover White
55 Azure Turqouise (lower)/Dover White
53 Glacier Blue (lower)/Dusk Blue
51 Dusk Blue (lower)/Glacier Blue
65 Olympic Gold (lower)/Dover White

OPTION IDENTIFICATION SYSTEM FOR THE 1969 CAMARO

Option #	Description
A01	Glass, tinted—all windows
A31	Window, power
A67	Seat, folding rear
*B37	Mats, floor
*B39	Guard, door edge
C05—AA	Top, convertible, white
C05—BB	Top, convertible, black
C06	Top, power convertible
C08—BB	Roof cover, vinyl—black
C08—CC	Roof cover, vinyl—blue (Dk)
C08—EE	Roof cover, vinyl—parchment
C08—FF	Roof cover, vinyl—brown
C08—SS	Roof cover, vinyl—Midnight green
+C50	Defroster, rear window
C60	Air conditioning
CE1	Headlight washer
+D33	Mirror, remote control, rearview
*D34	Mirror, visor vanity
D55	Console
D80	Spoiler
D90	Striping, sport
D96	Striping, fender
DX1	Striping, front accent
F41	Suspension, special purpose
G31	Spring, special rear
G76	Axle, rear 3.36 radio
G80	Axle, Positraction
G92	Axle, rear 3.08 ratio
G94	Axle, rear 3.31 ratio
G96	Axle, rear 3.55 ratio
G97	Axle, rear 2.73 ratio
GT1	Axle, rear 2.56 ratio
HO1	Axle, rear 3.07 ratio
J50	Brakes, power
J52	Brakes, power disc
JL8	Brakes, power disc 4 wheel
K02	Fan, radiator
K05	Heater, engine block

Option #	Description
K79	Generator, 42-amp
K85	Generator, 63-amp
KD5	Ventilation, HD closed engine positive
L22	Engine, 155-hp Turbo-Thrift 250-cu-in 6-cyl
L34	Engine, 350-hp Turbo-Jet 396-cu-in V8 (Camaro SS)
L35	Engine, 325-hp Turbo-Jet 396-cu-in V8 (Camaro SS)
L65	Engine, 250-hp Turbo-Fire 350 V8 396-cu-in V8 (Camaro SS)
L78	Engine, 375-hp Turbo-Jet 396-cu-in V8 (Camaro SS)
L89	Engine, 375-hp Turbo-Jet 396-cu-in V8 (Camaro SS)
M11	Shift lever, floor mounted
M20	Transmission, 4-speed wide-range
M21	Transmission, 4-speed close-ratio
M22	Transmission, 4-speed HD
M35	Transmission, Powerglide
M40	Transmission, Turbo Hydra-Matic
MB1	Transmission, Torque-Drive
MC1	Transmission, special 3-speed
N10	Exhaust, dual
N33	Steering wheel, Comfortilt
N34	Steering wheel, Sports-styled
N40	Steering, power
N44	Steering, special
N65	Tire, space-saver spare
N95	Wheel cover, simulated wire
N96	Wheel cover, mag-style
NC8	Exhaust system, chambered
P01	Wheel cover
P06	Wheel trim rings
PA2	Wheel cover, mag-spoke
PL5	Tire, F70 x 14 Original Equipment Blackwall with White Lettering

Option #	Description
PK8	Tire, E78 x 14 Original Equipment Whitewall
PW7	Tire, F70 x 14 Original Equipment White Stripe
PW8	Tire, F70 x 14 Original Equipment Red Stripe
PY4	Tire, F70-14 special "Belted" Original Equipment white stripe
PY5	Tire, F70-14 special "Belted" Original Equipment red stripe
T60	Battery, HD
U15	Speed warning indicator
U16	Gauge, Tachometer
U17	Instrumentation, special
+U35	Clock, electric
U46	Light monitoring system
U57	Stereo tape system
U63	Radio, pushbutton, AM
U69	Radio, pushbutton AM/FM
U73	Antenna, manual rear
U79	Radio, AM/FM stereo
U80	Speaker, rear
V01	Radiator, HD
*V31	Guard, bumper front
*V32	Guard, bumper rear
V75	Tire chain, liquid
VE3	Bumper, special front
YA1	Belts, Custom Deluxe
YA2	Belts, shoulder rear
YA3	Belts, shoulder front
Z21	Style Trim Group
Z22	Rally Sport
Z23	Special Interior
Z27	Camaro SS
Z28	Special Performance Package
Z87	Custom Interior
ZJ7	Wheels, Rally
ZJ9	Lighting, auxiliary
ZL2	Hood, Special Ducted
Z11	Pace Car

*Group ZPS   +Group ZQ2

1969 CAMARO POWER TEAMS

ENGINES	TRANSMISSIONS	REAR AXLE RATIO (:1)*			
		Std.	Optional		
			Econ.	Perf.	Spcl.
Standard Engines					
140-hp Turbo-Thrift 230 Six	3-Speed (2.85:1 Low)	3.08	2.73	3.36	
	4-Speed (2.85:1 Low)	3.08	2.73	3.36	
	Torque-Drive	2.73			
	Powerglide				
	Turbo Hydra-Matic	2.73	2.56	3.08	3.36
210-hp Turbo-Fire 327 V8	3-Speed (2.54:1 Low)	3.08	2.73	3.36	
	4-Speed (2.54:1 Low)	3.08	2.73	3.36	
	Powerglide				
	Turbo Hydra-Matic	2.73	2.56		3.36
Extra-Cost Engines					
155-hp Turbo-Thrift 250 Six	3-Speed (2.85:1 Low)	3.08	2.73	3.36	
	4-Speed (2.85:1 Low)	3.08	2.73	3.36	
	Torque-Drive	2.73			
	Powerglide				
	Turbo Hydra-Matic	2.73	2.56	3.08	3.36
255-hp Turbo-Fire 350 V8	Special 3-Speed (2.42:1 Low)	3.31	3.07	3.55	3.73
	4-Speed (2.52:1 Low)	3.31	3.07	3.55	3.73 / 4.10
	Powerglide	3.08	2.73	3.36	3.55
	Turbo Hydra-Matic				
300-hp Turbo-Fire 350 V8	Special 3-Speed (2.42:1 Low)				3.73
	4-Speed (2.52:1 Low)	3.31	3.07	3.55	3.73 / 4.10
	Powerglide	3.08	2.73	3.36	3.55
	Turbo Hydra-Matic				
325-hp Turbo-Jet 396 V8	Special 3-Speed (2.42:1 Low)	3.07	2.73	3.31	
	4-Speed (2.52:1 Low)	3.07	2.73	3.31	
	Turbo Hydra-Matic	3.07	2.73		2.56

*Positraction required for 3.73, 4.10; optional for all others. For ratios that apply to models with air conditioning, consult your dealer.

1969 Custom Feature Accessories (Available from Dealers)

"Four Season" Air Conditioning	Tachometer
Stereo tape player	Litter container
Stereo multiplex	Compass
Push-button AM radio	Underhood light
AM-FM radio	Luggage compartment light
Rear seat speaker	Glove compartment light
Wheel covers (3 types)	Ashtray light
Fender guards	Courtesy lights
Bumper guards	GM Vigilite (fibre optics, page 224)
Door edge guards	Locking as tank cap
Rear window defogger	Spare tire lock
Vanity visor mirror	Right-hand rear view mirror
Tissue dispenser	Fire extinguisher
Power brakes	Highway emergency kit
Electric clock	Child safety seat
Seat belt retractors	Cruise-master speed control
Hand portable spotlight	Rear deck lid luggage carrier
Rubber floor mats	Ski Rack
Engine block heater	Tape cartridge holder

Early Camaro advertisements dwelt repetitively with the "Hugger" theme, referrring apparently to Camaro's claimed ability to "hug" the road. However, this appelation appears generally to have been ignored by the buying public.

Camaro hugs the road. Squeezes the competition.

In introducing the new cowl induction hood, an attempt was made to tie it to the well-regarded SS configuration, and the name "Super Scoop" selected for promotion. However, like "Hugger", while apparently a good idea at the time, the alliterative name has not survived.

insert foot...

open mouth

Camaro's new Super Scoop.
Step on the gas and it steps up performance.

1969 SPORT COUPE

1969 Camaro Sport Coupe   *Courtesy Chevrolet, Vista, California*

1969 Camaro Sport Coupe

Mr. Gerry Tieri, Escondido, California

New front end appears wider with re-positioned parking lamps.

New black and silver egg crate grill appears move massive.

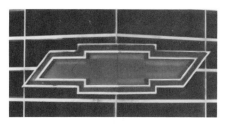

Chevrolet's familiar bow-tie emblem appears on grille of standard model.

Bright metal trim accents at headlamps are part of Style Trim option and are also included in Rally Sport.

New shape of wheel openings appears more advanced than semi-circular openings previously employed.

Rim-less round parking lamps are removed to location below front bumper. As in 1968, parking lights stay ON with headlights.

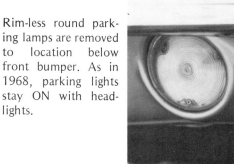

Clean lines of unchanged standard hood are carried forward into 1969.

Front header panel insignia is carried over from 1968.

Engine size, if V8, is indicated by appropriate insignia placed on front fenders along with standard side marker lights. 307 engine (on right side fender shown above), is a new engine, introduced in February of 1969, which replaced the 327 cu. in. version then discontinued.

Camaro script emblem appears again on front fender flanks.

Windshields are identical 1967-1969, but as noted previously, Convertible glass is 1" lower than Sport Coupe.

New wider mirror hangs from windshield header molding.

Standard Sport Coupe rain drip moldings are painted, but bright metal trim is furnished with the optional Rally Sport package.

Side window glass continues with slight curve adding to appearance.

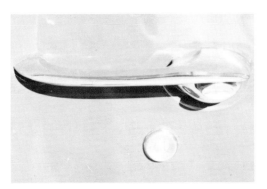

Chromed pushbutton outside door handles are unchanged.

Chromed door edge guards are part of optional Appearance Guard Group which also includes front and rear bumper guards, floor mats, and, in 1969, a visor vanity mirror.

Lower rocker panel trim strip is standard.

Rear quarter window has cushioned bright metal trim on forward edge providing an effective seal when both windows are raised.

Although their appearance is generally similar, the 1969 doors do not interchange with 1968. The position of the "crease" along side of car is raised, and inner and inside revisions are also made.

Revised wheel openings and repositioning of the side "crease" greatly changes the appearance in 1969.

Simulated rear wheel housing louvers are embossed into rear quarter.

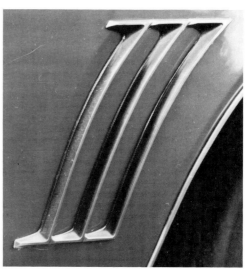

Louver trim plates are furnished as part of the Rally Sport package. An alternate Option, the Style Trim Group includes this trim, wheel opening moldings, black-painted lower body sill, and right headlight and taillight accents.

Wheel opening trim strips are also part of the optional Style Trim Group.

Rear window glass in Sport Coupe is unchanged from 1967-69.

Camaro emblem continues on rear deck lid.

Rear side marker lights are red, front ones amber.

Storage compartment is cramped with storage of standard spare tire. Optional space saver tire (page 227) improves situation.

Rear deck lid interchanges with earlier models.

Slightly flared fenders of earlier years (page 90) are replaced with clean lines of 1969 items.

Eliminated fuel filler cap between taillights is quick visible identification of 1969 model.

The fuel tank filler tube has been relocated to a position behind the rear license plate. Provided with a plain cap, it is reached by rotating the plate.

1967 Camaro Convertible

1967 Rally Sport Camaro Convertible

side rub strips are owner added

1967 Camaro SS350 with Rally Sport Option

1967 Camaro Sport Coupe

side rub strips are owner-added

1968 Camaro Convertible

1968 Camaro Sport Coupe

1968 Camaro SS Sport Coupe with Rally Sport option

1968
Camaro SS
Sport Coupe

1968 Camaro Sport Coupe with Rally Sport option

1968 Camaro Sport Coupe with Z28 option

1969 Camaro Sport Coupe with Rally Sport equipment

1969 Camaro Sport Coupe

1969 Camaro Sport Coupe with Style Trim Group

1969 Camaro Pace Car Convertible

1969 Camaro Sport Coupe with Z28 and black vinyl roof options.

Owner has repainted wheels to body color and added spoiler highlight stripe

1970 Camaro Sport Coupe with Z28 and Rally Sport options.

1970 Camaro Sport Coupe with Rally Sport Option

1970 Camaro Sport Coupe

1971 Camaro Sport Coupe

1972 Camaro Sport Coupe with Vinyl Roof Cover option

1973 Camaro Type LT with Rally Sport and Style Trim

1974 Camaro Sport Coupe

1974 Camaro Z28

1976 Camaro Sport Coupe

1976 Camaro Type LT

1977 Camaro Z28

1978 Camaro Type LT Coupe

1979 Camaro Z28

1979 Camaro Rally Sport

1981 Camaro Sport Coupe

New three-segment taillight lens is an obvious change for 1969.

Bow-tie emblem appears in center of rear panel replacing fuel filler cap.

The bright metal trim accents are part of the optional Style Trim group and are also included with the Rally Sport.

1969 RALLY SPORT

The 1969 Rally Sport option available on both Sport Coupe and Convertible includes: black-painted front grille with concealed headlights and headlight washers, fender striping (except when sport striping or Z28 is ordered), simulated rear fender louvers, front and rear wheel opening moldings, black body sill, RS emblem on grille, steering wheel and rear panel, Rally Sport front fender nameplates, bright accented taillights, back up lights below rear bumper, and bright roof drip molding on the Sport Coupe.

1969 Camaro Sport Coupe with Rally Sport option

Mr. Ernest Padgett, Vista, California

1969 RS grille, obvious for its concealed head lights, is black painted, lacks silver highlighting of standard grille (page 152).

Distincitve new RS letters appear on front grille.

Bright trim accents parking lights of RS, is not used on standard parking light lens (page 152).

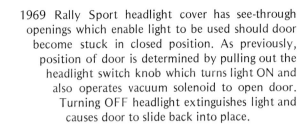

1969 Rally Sport headlight cover has see-through openings which enable light to be used should door become stuck in closed position. As previously, position of door is determined by pulling out the headlight switch knob which turns light ON and also operates vacuum solenoid to open door. Turning OFF headlight extinguishes light and causes door to slide back into place.

The Rally Sport headlight switch also controls vacuum operation of headlamp doors and includes switch and hose bibs as seen on lower switch.

New for 1969, headlight washers were a part of the Rally Sport option and also a separately available Option.

HEADLAMP WASHER INSTRUCTION

THIS VEHICLE IS EQUIPPED WITH A HEADLAMP WASHER SYSTEM THAT IS ACTIVATED BY THE WASHER-WIPER SWITCH. TO OPERATE THE SYSTEM DEPRESS THE WASHER BUTTON ALL THE WAY IN AND HOLD FOR A PERIOD OF TIME THAT WILL SUFFICIENTLY WASH THE HEADLAMP AND THEN RE-LEASE. WHEN OPERATING THIS WASHER SYSTEM THE WINDSHIELD WIPERS WILL BE IN MOTION SINCE THE WIPER MOTOR DRIVES THE WASHER PUMP THE WINDSHIELD WASHER SYSTEM IS ALSO OPERATED WITH WASHER WIPER SWITCH AS OUTLINED IN THE INSTRUCTION MANUAL PROCEDURE

NOTE:

THE HEADLAMP WASHER FUNCTIONS ONLY WHEN THE BUTTON IS DEPRESSED ON THE WASHER-WIPER SWITCH, THERE COULD BE AN OCCA-SION WHEN THE FLUID WILL ALSO WASH THE WINDSHIELD DEPENDING ON THE LENGTH OF TIME THE WASHER BUTTON IS DEPRESSED.

Instruction sheet for headlight washers was delivered with car.

Two chromed nozzles on each headlight flushed dirt from the lamps when windshield washer was operated.

"Rally-Sport" insignia again appears on fender flanks of cars equipped with that option.

The RS emblem appears at the hub of the steering wheel.

The standard embossed simulated louvers at the rear wheel openings are trimmed with a bright metal dress-up as part of the Rally Sport option.

Back up lights appear beneath bumpers on Rally Sport optioned cars; the rear spoiler is an additional Option frequently found on these cars.

Camaro's 18 gallon fuel tank is suspended at the rear beneath the floor of the luggage compartment. Large differential housing, used with heavier V8 engines, has 12 bolt cover.

RS option appears on both Sport Coupe and Convertible models.

Bright metal trim accents the RS taillights with horizontal
bar marking obvious change from standard lens (page 160).

Following continuing GM practice, model year again appears
on lens.

RS emblem on rear is new for 1968,
replacing special RS fuel filler cap used
previously (page 96).

1969 fuel filler cap is concealed behind
license plate.

The 1969 Convertible marked the end of a brief three year manufacturing span. Only 17,573 units were built, and at the end of the year, the Convertible model was dropped permanently from the Camaro line.

1969 Camaro Convertible with SS Option

The basic SS Option for 1969 includes the Turbo-Fire 350 engine with bright accents; power front disc brakes; floor-mounted 3-speed transmission; special hood; suspension, and ornamentation; sport striping; hood insulation; F70 x 14 white-lettered blackwall tires; 14 x 7 wheels, black-painted body sill, simulated rear louvers; SS emblems on fenders, grille, and rear panel.

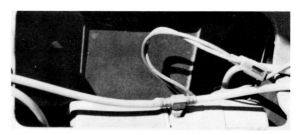

Electrically-operated hydraulic pump concealed behind rear seat operates hydraulic rams on each side to fold top mechanism.

Switch, recessed into instrument panel (not suspended beneath as previously), controls operation of top mechanism.

When not equipped with Power Top option, the Convertible is furnished with a plastic clip to hold top mechanism in lowered position.

1969

Photo courtesy Indianapolis Speedway Corporation

For the second time in only three years, the Camaro was chosen Pace Car for the Indianapolis 500 mile race.

In 1982, for the third time, a Camaro was chosen to pace the 500-Mile Race at Indianapolis. A specially-prepared silver-and-blue Z28, was selected to be powered by a 5.0 liter fuel-injected V8 engine derived from the production Cross-Fire V8. As previously, a limited number of Pace Car Replicas were later made available through Chevrolet Dealers.

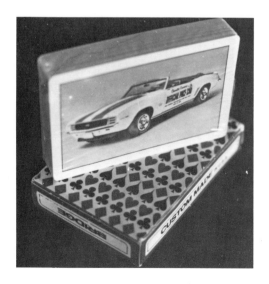

Many commemorative items were produced in connection with the 1969 Pace Car, among them were handsome sets of playing cards.

Why is the Cam

Camaro has been named the Official Pace Car in the Indianapolis 500 for the second time in three years—a 50-year record! If you haven't driven the Hugger, take a

hi
the
th

1969 Pace Car Convertible promotional models are nicely detailed, but lack distinctive striping.

AMT produced a kit model of the 1969 Camaro which could be built as the Pace Car, as a Custom model, or drag car.

Camaro SS Convertible with Rally Sport equipment and new air intake hood.

e pace car again?   Because it's *the Hugger.*

MARK OF EXCELLENCE

at Indy. Maybe ng you don't. t it takes. Again pack at Indy. t with a 300-hp

350-cu.-in. V8 and run up through a 325-hp 396-cu.-in. job. There's even a new hood you can order with a super scoop intake that opens on acceleration, ramming cooler air into the

engine for more power.
   This Hugger offers the widest tread of any sportster at its price. It comes on strong with wide oval tires on 14 x 7-inch-wide wheels and a beefed-up

suspension.
   The transmission is a special 3-speed floor shift. For those who want still more, there's a 4-speed available with a Hurst shifter.

Indy's tough. So's Camaro SS. When it comes to pacesetting, Camaro knows its way around. **CHEVROLET**

Putting you first, keeps us first.

This attractive advertisement appeared in full color in the centerfold of the Official Program for the 53rd Indianapolis 500 race, held on May 30, 1969.

1969 PACE CAR CONVERTIBLE

Following selection of the 1969 Camaro Convertible as Pace Car for the Indianapolis 500 race, an Option was made available for those wishing to obtain a replica. The original Pace Car (actually there were at least 2 at Indianapolis), was simply a blueprinted version of a stock Camaro with a 375 HP 396 cu. in. engine and Turbo Hydra-Matic transmission! Fitted with 15 x 7 wheels, heavy duty battery, alternator, and radiator, little else was done to the car that would easily run at 130 mph setting the starting pace. Thus, while not exactly as the original, the "Pace Car Convertibles" as the replicas have come to be known were ordered with the following minimum added Options:

Option #	Item	Retail Cost
50	Color—Dover White	n/c
720	Orange houndstooth trim	n/c
AA	White top	n/c
Z27	Camaro SS Option	$224.96
Z87	Custom Interior	79.80
Z22	Rally Sport Option	95.00
YA	Custom Deluxe seat belts	6.46
ZL2	Special Ducted Hood	57.00
D80	Rear Spoiler	23.56
ZJ7	Rally Wheels	25.84
Z11	Indy pole car accents (striping; orange boot; etc.)	26.60

According to Chevrolet records, a total of only 3675 of these Model 12467 Camaro Convertible Pace Car replicas were built, all at their Norwood Assembly Plant. Each bears the special identification Z11 on its body plate (see next page), and can thus be positively identified. In addition, an unspecified number of similarly equipped Convertibles were assembled in the Van Nuys Assembly Plant, but since they do not carry the Z11 number on their body plate, can easily be distinguished from the Norwood cars.

Chevrolet held special "Pacesetter-Values" sales in which Camaro was offered at $147 less than the 1968 model with comparable equipment; other lines including Nova, Malibu, and Impala were also featured in booklet deriving interest from Camaro's selection as Indianapolis Pace Car.

Pacesetter Values
on the cars that set the pace.

Three surviving 1969 Pace Car Convertibles were assembled for 1981 photograph.

1969 Indy 500 Pace Car

1969 PACE CAR CONVERTIBLE

All 3675 Pace Car Convertibles assembled at Norwood plant have Z11 designation on their body plates (right); similar cars from the Van Nuys plant (below) do not.

The mandatory special ducted hood includes air cleaner with built-in hood seal.

The insulated underside of hood has incoming air chamber shaped to match seal on air cleaner.

Stripe pattern is same as on Z28, but its orange color is limited to Pace Car.

Rear of ducted hood forms an inverted scoop to force air into carburetor when accelerator linkage-operated butterfly valve beneath lip is opened.

SS letters on fender flanks are now separate letters unlike earlier one-piece emblem (page 109).

SS letters are repeated on rear.

Spoiler is standard on Pace Car Convertible, a mandatory Option.

Sport striping of fenders is part of mandatory Rally Sport Option. 14'' Rally Wheels are also mandatory option.

1969 PACE CAR CONVERTIBLE

Orange and black houndstooth cloth with orange vinyl trim are exclusive to the Pace Car Convertible. Also available in similar seat coverings for other models are similar black & white and black & yellow combinations.

Custom Deluxe seat belts are mandatory Option.

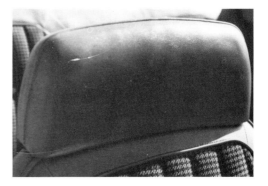

Adjustable head rest is orange to match seat color.

Other than exclusive color combination, seats are same as conventional 1969 Custom Interior.

White top is mandatory selection for Pace Car Convertible.

Convertible windshield headers, initially bright chrome in 1967, were toned down to a brushed aluminum finish in 1968 as part of non-glare safety-oriented redesign.

All Camaro Convertible top boots are secured to the body by plastic clips which snap over bright metal trim around top well.

The Pace Car Convertible has orange vinyl boot, unique to this model.

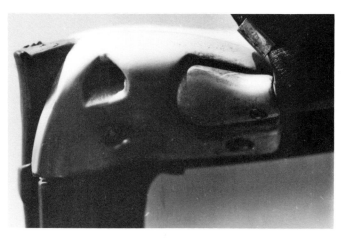

Rear view mirror is suspended from header by bracket trimmed with plastic shroud.

Adjustable sun visors are supported by chromed brackets at the windshield upper corners.

Two sun visors are supplied in all models; vinyl covered in Convertibles, cloth in Sport Coupes.

Convertible's windshield pillars are trimmed with bright metal.

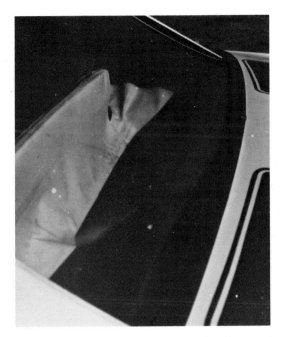

Clear plastic rear window is sewn in place and cannot be lowered separately.

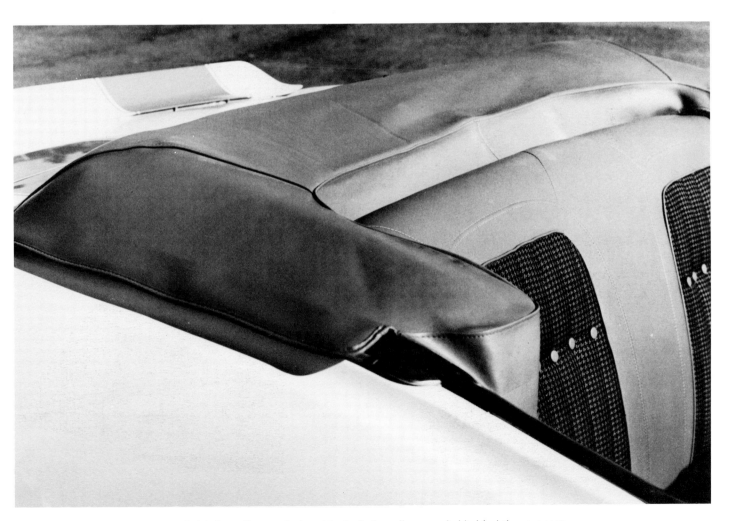

Folded top fits neatly into black cloth well suspended behind the rear seat.

Ash trays are located in each of the two rear seat arm rests.

A feature of all Camaro Convertibles is the arm rest to be found on either side. Only with the optional Custom Interior are these to be found in the Sport Coupe.

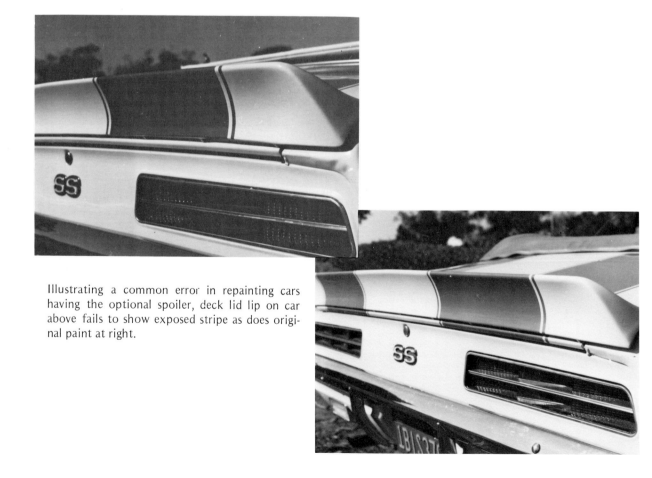

Illustrating a common error in repainting cars having the optional spoiler, deck lid lip on car above fails to show exposed stripe as does original paint at right.

Lacking the added rigidity supplied by a continuous steel roof, the Convertible body tends to flex under running loads. To reduce this twist, four cylindrical counterweights are installed in the front and rear corners of these cars. Spring-loaded counterweights, operating in this fluid-filled damper, greatly reduce the problem, but add about 100 pounds of dead weight.

1969 Z28

"You can build your Camaro from an economical family car all the way to a spirted sportster with a name to match: Z28."
... 1969 Camaro Sales Folder

Technically ordered as Option Z28, the Special Performance Package, available on Sport Coupes only, included the 302 cu. in. V8 engine with bright accents; dual exhausts; Z28 emblems on grille, front fender and rear panel; special front and rear suspension; rear bumper guards; heavy duty radiator and temperature-controlled fan; quick ratio steering; 15 x 7" wheels with center caps and trim rings; E70 x 15 white lettered blackwall tires; auxiliary front valance panel and rear deck spoiler, plus special paint stripes on hood and rear deck.

The Z28 Option was only available when tachometer or Special Instrumentation, 4-speed transmission, power front or 4-wheel disc brakes were also ordered, and Positraction was a recommended additional Option.

1969 Camaro Sport Coupe with Z28 Option

Emblem appears on
front grille.

Mr. Bill Ferguson, Escondido, California

Missing from this car is a standard lower front spoiler which was a part of the 1969 Z28 Option. See page 223 for this item.

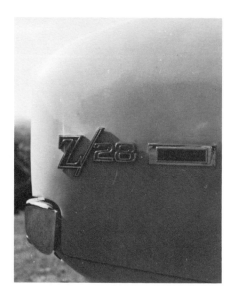

Z28 insignia appears on front fenders in place of engine size as previously (page 118).

Wider 15 x 7" wheels replace the 6" wheels of 1968, but there is little difference in appearance.

Standard hood displays distinctive stripe pattern, mark of the Z28. Virtually exclusive to that model, it was used elsewhere only on the 1969 Pace Car, and then in orange only.

The 302 emblem appears on sides of the air tunnel of the optional ducted hood on Z28.

An alternate hood, the optional Special Ducted Hood, was offered on both Z28 and the SS models.

1969 Z28

Cast aluminum ribbed rocker arm covers appear as part of the bright accent dress up of the 302 engine in 1969 replacing earlier chromed covers.

Matched Sports type rear view mirrors are an aftermarket accessory; only the conventional mirror on drivers side was standard.

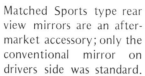

Z28 emblem appears on rear panel.

White portion of lens accommodates integral back up light.

Standard 1969 taillight is unchanged.

Rear deck spoiler is standard part of 1969 Z28 option.

207

Camaro nameplate appears on door
above door pull.

Chromed plastic door lock knobs
appear on doors in 1969.

Inside door latch release rotates from front of
arm rest.

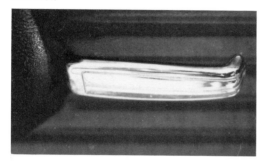

STANDARD DOOR PANEL

Window riser crank knobs are translucent
plastic.

1969 Camaro standard inside door panel.

Camaro script appears on door forward of door pull.

A strap type door pull is provided.

Translucent crank knobs and chromed inside door lock knobs are also used on Custom Interior panels.

Inside door latch release pivots outward from recessed well.

CUSTOM INTERIOR DOOR PANEL

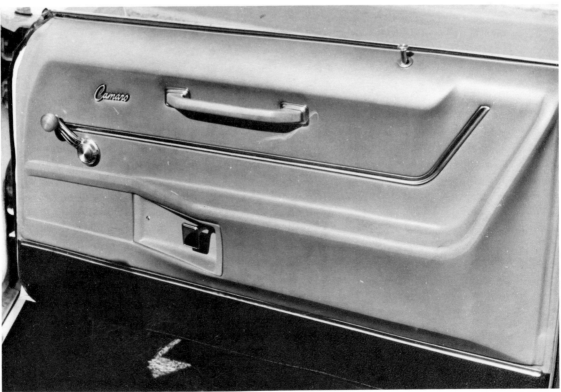

1969 Custom Interior inside door panel.

Rear seat of Sport Coupe with standard interior lacks arm rests or ash trays.

Standard 1969 seat has horizontal stripe insert panel. Seats are available in vinyl only.

Adjustable head restraints are supplied on all front seats, standard as well as Custom Interior.

Height of adjustable head rest is maintained by spring-loaded latch on seat top.

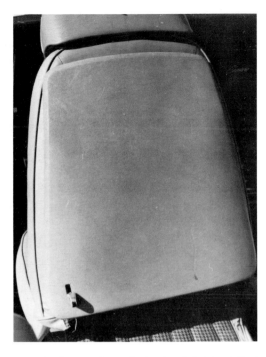

Seat back latch knob
is chromed.

Seat backs are formed plastic. A latch at their
lower outside corner releases back and allows
access to the rear.

Rear seats of Convertibles, both standard and also
Custom Interior, have arm rests at either end.

Custom Interior seats are available in both all-vinyl, and
also vinyl-and-cloth trim. Colors of houndstooth cloth
include black/white, ivory/black, yellow/black, and
orange/black.

Distinctive trim of Custom Interior includes seven upholstery buttons on the back of each of four seats.

Again in 1969 a Folding Rear Seat Option was offered in both Sport Coupe and Convertible. Much like the 1968 similar seat, it offered increased package carrying space at modest added cost. Curiously, according to Chevrolet records, this Option was not available in the 1969 Pace Car Convertibles.

Camaro insignia appears at center of standard steering wheel.

SS or RS insignia, as applicable, will appear at hub of steering wheel.

New for 1969, replacing earlier three-spoke wheels, is this two-spoke wheel with padded hub.

The Sports-Styled Steering Wheel is one Option for 1969; another is similar cushioned-rim wheel.

Large single pedal operates brake in automatic-equipped cars. Dual smaller pedals (right) are for manual transmission cars.

Optional wheel's horn button will bear RS or SS emblem as applicable.

Four-speed shift pattern appears on console. Other interchangeable plates display alternate patterns.

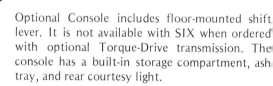

Optional Console includes floor-mounted shift lever. It is not available with SIX when ordered with optional Torque-Drive transmission. The console has a built-in storage compartment, ash tray, and rear courtesy light.

Special Instrumentation Option is available on V8 models only. It includes ammeter, temperature, oil pressure, and fuel guages on the console, and electric clock and tachometer in the instrument panel cluster.

The console also features a storage compartment for unused front seat belt buckles.

A new locking steering column provides security and places ignition switch on the column.

New larger head keys are provided replacing the earlier style (left).

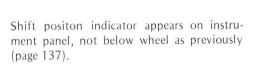

Shift positon indicator appears on instrument panel, not below wheel as previously (page 137).

Standard transmission shift lever location, remains on the column; floor-mounts are options except for 4-speed.

Disc brake Option is indicated on brake pedal.

Bright metal pedal trim is part of Custom Interior Option.

1969 instrument cluster houses all instruments.

New rectangular Astro Ventilation vents are placed at ends of instrument panel.

120 mph speedometer is recessed deeply in cluster.

Lights beneath speedometer display Left Turn arrow, FUEL (only illuminated with Special Instrumentation Option), BRAKE, and BRIGHT.

Vents at upper center of panel are provided with air conditioning Option only.

Two separate sliding controls on the cowl panels direct air flow through lower and also upper vent outlets.

Lights and windshield wiper/washer are controlled at lower left side of instrument panel.

Standard cluster has Camaro insignia on solid panel; Optional electric clock requires different cluster as its supports are molded-in.

Appearance of fuel gauge matches that of speedometer, but needle travels only through about 90 degrees.

Lights below fuel gauge display GEN, TEMP, OIL, and right turn arrow.

Anntennas are supplied with optional radios AM-FM fixed length antenna is on left, standard collapsible on right.

Optional AM-FM radio face rotates with sliding bar switch to display appropriate scale.

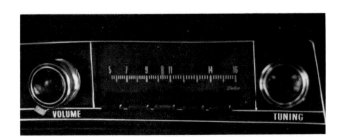

Optional AM radio has fixed tuning scale.

Standard heater control panel includes a switch position (AIR) for incoming ventilating air.

1969 Instrument panel. Wood-trim accents are part of the Custom Interior option.

Chromed knob is original, but it shortly was replaced with a black plastic knob (right) to reduce costs.

Optional 4-speed transmission is floor-mounted with standard rubber boot seal.

1969 4-speed transmission was supplied by Hurst whose name appears on the lever.

Standard Camaro script normally appears above ashtray.

Optional Four Seasons air conditioning provides outlet vents in upper center of instrument panel. Camaro script appears above glove box door.

Ash tray at lower center of panel rotates open; contains tray and lighter.

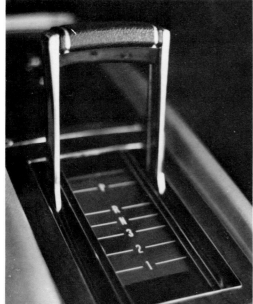

For 1969, Turbo Hydra-Matic optional automatic transmission became available on *all* engines except the 302. Powerglide remained a less costly alternative Option on the SIX, the 307, and the 350 cu. in. engines.

Air conditioning compressor and hoses appear under the hood.

All Camaro bodies are built by Fisher Body Divison. Each bears a Body Tag on the cowl at the left side and can be easily seen when the hood is raised. Tag bears information regarding Model Year, Series, Assembly Plant location, Unit number, Trim, and Paint color, etc.

Standard air cleaner for the Special Performance Z28 option is open sided, chromed cover.

Standard V8 air cleaner has enclosed air filter with controlled-inlet air intake.

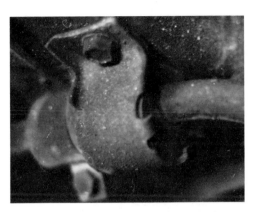

Standard 11/16" front stabilizer bar is secured to the lower suspension arms.

Left side shock absorber is mounted behind the axle; right side, ahead. Staggering the shocks in this manner reduced tendency for axle to raise under acceleration.

Several striping Options were avaiable. This is the "DX1" Front Accent Striping motif in which the front header panel stripe of former years parts at the hood center and narrows to a point near the cowl, and parts at the sides to accommodate the engine size emblem. See pages 223 and 229 for other options.

Rear spoiler is an available Option, but is a standard part of the Z28 option.

The standard short rear bumper guards (above) are replaced with larger guards (right) as part of the optional Appearance Guard Group. These are also included in the Z28 Special Performance option.

Alternate 1969 fender striping includes this type which is part of the Rally Sport or the Style Trim optional groups, but could be ordered separately as RPO D96.

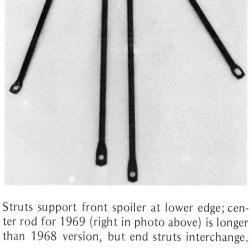

Struts support front spoiler at lower edge; center rod for 1969 (right in photo above) is longer than 1968 version, but end struts interchange.

The lower front spoiler is included with the rear deck spoiler as a single Option. Both are included in the Special Performance Z28 option.

Substantial change in appearance occurs with the use of optional Endura bumper (above) which replaces the conventional chromed type. No bumper guards are available for this painted option.

The optional vinyl roof cover is available on the sport Coupe only and includes the bright metal outline moldings. Five colors were available; black, blue, parchment, midnight green, and brown.

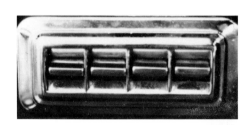

Another available Option was power-operated windows. All four side windows were controlled from a switch panel on the driver's door, and individual switches (right) were placed beneath the other three windows.

The optional Light Monitoring System included sensors on the front and rear lights that through a system of flexible fiber-optic tubes displayed this information. Chromed displays were mounted on each front fender and on the rear package tray there to be visible in the rear view mirror. These displayed functioning lights and operating turn signals.

Optional Special Ducted Hood collects air at the pressure area below the windshield and by means of an accelerator linkage-controlled flutter valve directs it to the carburetor.

Built-in tunnel directs air to top of carburetor intake (see page 194).

Electrically operated flutter valve is at forward end of overhang.

Rubber-sealed air intake mates with underside of hood and accepts incoming air when flutter valve is opened.

Decal indicates rear of rubber sealing ring.

Two spacers are available, the higher one for standard engine installations, a shorter one to allow for the greater height of the Z28 aluminum intake manifold.

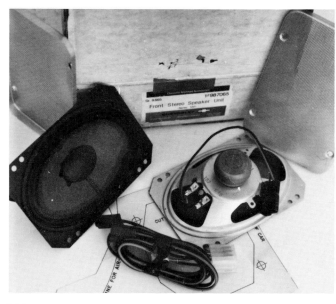

This Stereo Speaker Kit was available at the Dealer's and would be required for the installation of the stereo multiplex AM-FM radio. An additional kit is necessary to complete the installation as full system has four speakers cross-wired for best effect.

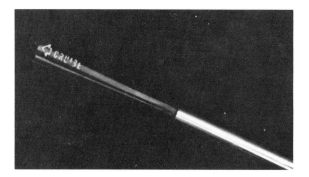

Optional Cruise-Master speed control, a Custom Feature Accessory, was installed by Dealers. System maintains preset speed until automatically disengaged when brake pedal is applied.

6000 redline, 7000 max. optional tachometer.

The Speed Warning Indicator, an available Option, sounded a buzzer when preset speed was exceeded.

6000 red line, 8000 max. optional tachometer.

5500 redline, 7000 max. optional tachometer.

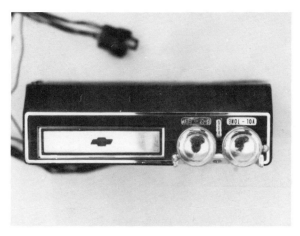

Optional Stereo Tape System which was suspended beneath the instrument panel included 4 speakers. It was not available when console with stereo radio was also ordered.

1969 AM-FM Stereo radio was actually composed of two chassis, an AM/FM monaural radio, and a separate multiplex adaptor mounted behind the instrument panel. Four speakers were employed, wired right front/left rear and converse for best stereo effect.

The Space Save Spare Tire was an option greatly appreciated by those who need added storage space. A cannister was supplied with mounted tire to inflate it when required.

The 1970 model year provides the basis for confusion. For a variety of reason, the "new" body style was not available at the start of what would otherwise have been the 1970 model year. Thus, Camaro continued the earlier body style, identifying these cars as 1970 models, until the car that would be later called the "1970½" model was ready. This later body style was announced on February 13, 1970, but cars did not go on sale until February 26th. Until that date, the "early 1970" models continued to be simply 1969 models re-identified.

1970 Camaro SS. The unique striping was an Option reserved for the Camaro SS when ordered with Rally Sport or Style Trim Group.

228

Camaro's commodious engine compartment permitted installation of larger-than-stock engines. From 1967 on, the 427 cu. in. engine was a popular power source for Dealers who then promoted their product in ads such as these. Chevrolet itself built 50 cars in 1969 with a 425 horsepower triple-carburetored version of the 427 cu. in. aluminum block engine. All of these cars, however, were race-orientated, few were seen on the street. Known as the ZL-1, these cars, like the Dealers' cars, were fast, solid racing cars; few were ever seen on the street.

Motion Performance Inc., an affiliate of Baldwin Chevrolet, a Dealer on Long Island, marketed the Phase III 454 Camaro, an even more potent mutant.

With its first new body in three years, Camaro assumed an appearance that it would retain for the next eleven. Wider and cleaner in appearance, the former quarter windows were eliminated and a new door gave greater accessiblity to the rear seats which were now formed to resemble bucket seats. A new wraparound instrument panel and standard front disc brakes were features, and exterior colors now totaled 15!

Daytona Yellow	Shadow Grey	Cortez Silver
Astro Blue	Citrus Green	Hugger Orange
Mulsanne Blue	Forest Green	Classic White
Classic Copper	Green Mist	Desert Sand
Autumn Gold	Cranberry Red	Camaro Gold

Dealer installed Custom Feature Accessories available for 1970:

Four Season air conditioning	Rear window defogger
AM push-button radio	Liquid tire chain dispenser
AM radio with tape player	Electric clock
AM-FM radio	Wheel covers (3 types)
AM-FM stereo radio	Rear deck luggage carrier
Rear seat speaker	Ski rack
Tape cartridge holder	Luggage compartment light
Fender guards	Courtesy lights
Vanity visor mirror	Underhood light
Tissue dispenser	Glove compartment light
Rear bumper guards	Highway emergency kit
Auto compass	Fire extinguisher
Right hand rear view mirror	Rubber floor mats
Door edge guards	Engine block heater
Litter container	Child & Infant safety seats
	Locking gas cap

CAMARO POWER TEAMS						
ENGINES	TRANSMISSIONS	REAR AXLE RATIOS	COMPRESSION RATIO	TORQUE	CARBURETION	REQUIRED FUEL
STANDARD ENGINES						
155-hp Turbo Thrift 250 Six	3-Speed	3.08	8.5:1	235 lb-ft. @ 1600 rpm	Single barrel	Regular
	Powerglide	2.73				
200-hp Turbo-Fire 307 V8	3-Speed	3.08	9.0:1	300 lb-ft. @ 2400 rpm	Two barrel	Regular
	Powerglide	2.73				
	Turbo Hydra-matic	2.73				
EXTRA-COST ENGINES						
250-hp Turbo-Fire 350 V8	4-Speed	3.36	9.0:1	345 lb-ft. @ 2800 rpm	Two barrel	Regular
	Turbo Hydra-matic	2.73				
300-hp Turbo-Fire 350 V8 (SS only)	4-Speed	3.31	10.25:1	380 lb-ft. @ 3200 rpm	Four barrel	Premium
	Turbo Hydra-matic	3.07				
360-hp Turbo-Fire 350 V8 (Z28 only)	4-Speed	3.73 or Special Option 4.10	11.00:1	380 lb-ft. @ 4500 rpm	Four barrel	Premium
350-hp Turbo-Jet 396 V8 (SS only)	4-Speed	3.31	10.25:1	415 lb-ft. @ 3400 rpm	Four barrel	Premium
	Turbo Hydra-matic					

The SS Option for 1970 includes as standard the 300 HP 350 cu. in. V8 with 4-V carburetor and dual exhausts and mandatory 4-speed or Turbo Hydra-matic; 396 cu. in. engine is optional. Hood insulation and black-painted grille and back panel are standard; also white-lettered F70 x 14 tires on 7" wheels; power assisted front disc brakes; and distinctive SS grille emblem. With the optional 396 engine, a special suspension and rear sway bar are included.

1970 Camaro SS Sport Coupe   *Mr. Gary Weathers, National City, California*

The Z28 for 1970 includes a new engine, the high performance 360 horsepower version of the 350 cu. in. Turbo-Fire V8. With mechanical lifters and a big 4V carburetor, it also has aluminum pistons and large valves along with a temperature-controlled fan. Available with either a 4-speed Hurst shifter or with Turbo Hydra-matic, it has front and rear stabilizer bars, and stiffer springs with matching shock absorbers as well as quick-ratio steering. White lettered F60 x 15 tires on 15" wheels are standard as is a heavy-duty radiator and special Z28 striping. Again in 1970, the rear spoiler is standard.

1970 Camaro Z28   *Mr. Carlos Rosete, Santee, California*

The Rally Sport Option for 1970 includes a black-out front grille with a color-matched resilient frame to act as a bumper, and a vertical bar down the middle of the grille. Split bumpers and rally-styled parking lights which stay on with the headlights are also added. Concealed windshield wipers and an RS on the steering wheel are standard with the option.

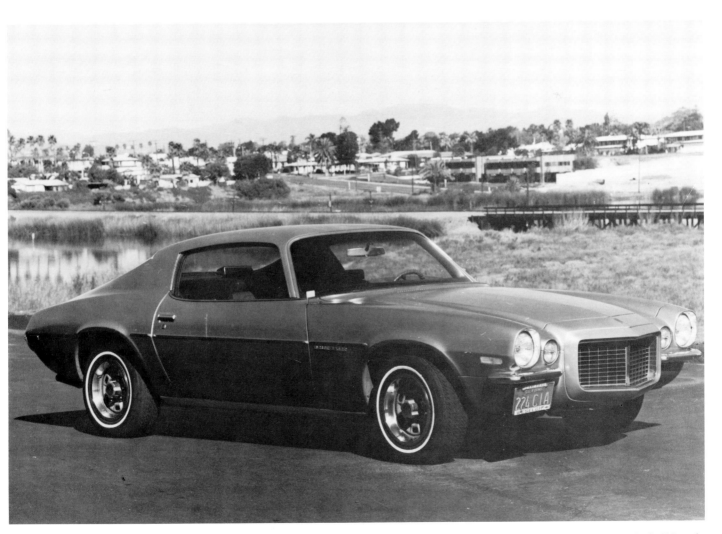

1970 Camaro Rally Sport

Mrs. Pauline Scott, Carlsbad, California

Full-width bumper is standard.

Standard side marker lights are continued

Full width standard bumper is replaced with resilient color-matched grille frame and short bumpers on Rally Sport.

Standard parking/directional lights appear beneath the bumper on Sport Coupe.

In the Rally Sport Option, new rally-styled parking lights are set between high intensity headlights; those below bumper deleted.

Hide-A-Way windshield wipers slip down behind up-lifted rear edge of hood on RS and SS options.

The new windshield is almost 4" wider, over 5" higher than the earlier style.

A new Camaro insignia appears on the front header panel.

The inside rear view mirror is bonded to the windshield, not suspended from the header as previously.

1970

Rear quarter windows have been eliminated and door top curved for better effect.

Astro Ventilation outlet vents are continued in door jamb.

New pull-type door handles appear; a color-matched decal is optional, as are door edge guards.

Camaro script in fender flanks is standard, V8 engine size indicated when applicable. Both are replaced with new upper-case lettered RALLY SPORT emblem (compare page 182).

Doors have been widened by almost 7", allowing greater access to the rear seats.

Distincive RS parking lights are placed inboard of head-lights.

Bright-metal trimmed new rear window is faired into the body contour.

Wheel well openings have built-in flare to accommodate wider tires.

The familiar Camaro script emblem again appears on the rear deck lid.

Side marker lights, a safety feature, are continued at both front and rear.

New round taillights include back up light in inner lamp.

Rear bumper is full width on all models.

1970 Z28

Z28 is an Option that can appear with standard or Rally Sport additional option. This car is rally sport Z28.

The RS option includes this color-matched resilient bumper.

Familiar Z28 emblem appears on conventional RS grille.

Also a part of the Rally Sport option, not Z28, are the short bumpers and parking lights that glow yellow along with the high intensity headlights.

Amber front marker lights are standard on all 1970 models.

Distinctive Z28 stripe pattern is similar to earlier style in front.

Z28 emblem appears on fender flanks. Rub strip is owner-added aftermarket accessory.

The revised stripe pattern no longer goes down over the rear deck lip (page 200) as it did previously.

Black-painted rear panel is normally part of the SS option, but looks especially good on Z28.

Rear deck spoiler is included as standard in the Z28 Option.

New 1970 hood continues to be hinged at the rear, opens at the front.

A push button latch is added to the 1970 console's storage compartment.

Recessed compartment has friction load to hold unused seat belt buckles in place of blades found in the earlier style.

The new optional console is higher, providing convenient arm rest.

Recessed door latch handle pivots outward.

Window crank handles are chromed; knobs are plastic.

Inside door panel features molded full-length arm rest. Lower portion is carpeted on optional Custom Interior.

Standard interior (above) is available in solid colors only. Custom Interior seats (right), in addition to having differing pattern, are available in solid or one of three two-tone combinations.

New adjustable head rests, having a more rectangular appearance than the earlier style, appear for 1970.

New optional streamlined sport mirror has inside remote control on driver's side. A chromed unit (page 249) is standard.

AM pushbutton radio or AM-FM radio, both Options, come with new hairline antenna built into the windshield glass.

A matching right side rear view mirror is also an optional item.

Attractive two-spoke steering wheel is standard.

Camaro emblem appears on steering wheel hub unless RS option is ordered.

Windshield wiper/ washer switch is located at left side.

New instrument cluster features wrap-around visibility. Tachometer is part of Special Instrumentation Group which also includes temperature gauge, ammeter, and clock.

A new 150 mph speedometer is standard.

New matching fuel gauge appears at right of speedometer.

Cigarette lighter is standard at right of instrument panel. Control for optional rear window defogger would be placed in indent beneath.

Center vent is provided with optional Four-Season air conditioning only.

Standard heater control at panel lower left would be replaced with Optional air conditioning control.

Standard adjustable vents at ends of instrument panel provide ventilation.

Automatic transmission shift pattern appears between large gauges.

Blanking plate is used with manual transmissions.

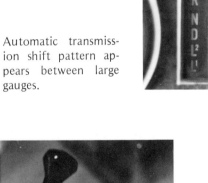

Spherical 4-speed knob bears shift pattern.

Standard Powerglide shift is placed on the column; floor shifts (right) are Options, but standard with Turbo Hydra-matic.

Hurst 4-speed transmission is one alternate option on extra-cost engines, Turbo Hydra-matic the other.

Camaro

1971 Sport Coupe/RS/SS/Z28

1971 Exterior colors include:

Tuxedo Black	*Lime Green*	*Rosewood Metallic*
Mulsanne Blue	*Cottonwood Green*	*Sandalwood*
Ascot Blue	*Antique Green*	*Nevada Silver*
Classic Copper	*Burnt Orange*	*Antique White*
Placer Gold	*Cranberry Red*	*Sunflower Yellow*

The closest thing to a Vette yet.

The 1971 Camaro was little changed from the 1970 model. Front seats now had integral head restraints, but that was about the only obvious change for the year. Under the hood though, it was a different matter. All Camaro engines had now been designed to operate on the new no-lead or low-lead gasolines. Compression ratios had been lowered on all engines except the basic SIX which remained at 8.5:1, but even that engine lost about 2% of its rated horsepower. The greatest change here was in the Z28's Turbo-Fire 350 which went from a rated 360 hp in 1970 to 330 in 1971, a drop of almost 10% with its compress ratio dropping from 11.0:1 in 1970 to 9.0:1 in 1971.

The Z28 was continued as a Performance car, but it had not the power and response that it did previously. Its appearance was substantially the same except that the standard "low" rear deck spoiler (page 238) could now be replaced with an optional "Big" spoiler (page 262), and few cars did not have the larger unit. The Special Instrumentation Group which included the tachometer and gauges for temperature and ammeter were standard with the Z28 as were the big F60 x 15 white-lettered tires on 15" special wheels. A new flat-topped black plastic shift knob came with the 4-speed transmission.

The RS Option was unchanged, featuring the black-out grill with surrounding resilient bumper and short bumpers at the sides. Again it included the rally-styled lights between the headlights and special identifications on the fender flanks and steering wheel.

The SS Option also remained substantially unchanged, and featured a 270 hp (down from 1970's 300 hp) 350 cu. in. V8 with 4V carburetor and dual exhausts. Optional 300 hp Turbo-Jet 396 V8 (down from 350 hp in 1970) added a special suspension including a rear stabilizer bar. With the SS came underhood insulation, black-painted grille and back panel, and F70 x 14 times on 7" rally wheels. Both the RS and the SS options also featured the Hide-A-Way windshield wipers.

CAMARO POWER TEAMS**					
	TRANSMISSIONS	REAR AXLE RATIOS	COMPRESSION RATIO	GROSS TORQUE	CARBURETION
STANDARD ENGINES					
145-hp (110-hp*) Turbo Thrift 250 Six	3-Speed	3.08	8.5:1	230 lb-ft/1600 rpm (185/1600*)	Single-barrel
	Powerglide	3.08			
200-hp (140-hp*) Turbo-Fire 307 V8	3-Speed	3.08	8.5:1	300 lb-ft/2400 rpm (235/2400*)	Two-barrel
	Powerglide	3.08			
	Turbo Hydra-matic	2.73			
AVAILABLE ENGINES					
245-hp (165-hp*) Turbo-Fire 350	4-Speed	3.08	8.5:1	350 lb-ft/2800 rpm (280/2400*)	Two-barrel
	Turbo Hydra-matic	2.73			
270-hp (210-hp*) Turbo-Fire 350 V8 (SS only)	4-Speed	3.42	8.5:1	360 lb-ft/3200 rpm (300/2800*)	Four-barrel
	Turbo Hydra-matic	3.08			
330-hp (275-hp*) Turbo-Fire 350 V8 (Z28 only)	4-Speed	3.73 or Special Option 4.10	9.0:1	360 lb-ft/4000 rpm (300/4000*)	Four-barrel
	Turbo Hydra-matic				
300-hp (260-hp*) Turbo-Jet 396 V8 (SS only)	4-Speed	3.42	8.5:1	400 lb-ft/3200 rpm (345/3200*)	Four-barrel
	Turbo Hydra-matic				

*SAE net (as installed) rating.
**For 1971, all Camaro engines have been designed to operate efficiently on the new no-lead or low-lead gasolines. In addition to the lower exhaust emissions attainable with this engine fuel combination, there are benefits in longer life for your spark plugs, exhaust system and other engine components. If these no-lead, low-lead gasolines are not available, any leaded regular grade gasoline with a research octane number of 91 or higher may be used.

1971 Camaro Sport Coupe

Mr. Claude Hollis, Spring Valley, California

Styled insignia appears on the front header panel.

Only one hood is offered with the new body style, but the SS Option adds an insulation underneath.

Sport Coupe's front bumper wraps around front corners.

Power-Beam sealed beam headlamps are standard. Bright metal ring frames lights.

The standard grille is high lighted with silver; full width front bumper has standard short lower guards.

Sport Coupe parking lights are placed in valance panel beneath full-width bumper.

Standard Sport Coupe has conventional visible windshield wipers, lacks bright metal trim at rear of hood (page 233). Hide-A-Way wipers are feature of optional RS or SS only.

Chromed outside rear view mirror is standard; sports-styled (page 241) is Option.

Door handles are unchanged. Color-matched decal is part of optional Style Trim Group which also includes bright accent around windows and parking and taillights.

Camaro script, new in 1970, appears on fender flanks.

Mirror is standard, but bright trim around side windows is optional.

This is the standard roof treatment. A Vinyl Roof Cover option is available in black, white, dark blue, dark brown, or dark green.

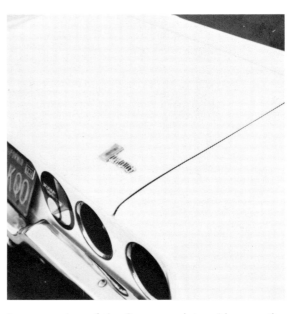

A new version of the Camaro script emblem continues on the rear deck lid.

Outer taillight lens is all-red; inner lens has white center for back-up lights. Bright metal trim around these lights is part of optional Style Trim Group.

Rear bumper is full width and wraps around corners as does front bumper.

Standard interiors are all-vinyl and are available in black, blue, jade, saddle, or sandlewood. The Custom Interior option is available in five color combinations of cloth-and-vinyl: black, black/blue, black/jade, saddle, or black/white.

Rear seats are again upholstered to simulate two bucket seats.

A new Camaro script appears on the steering wheel spoke replacing the Chevrolet bow-tie used in 1970 (page 241).

New deep-foam, high-back bucket front seats appear for 1971 replacing earlier seats with adjustable head restraints.

1972 Camaro.
If you're looking for the closest thing to a Vette yet, you've come to the right catalog.

1972 exterior colors include:

Mulsanne Blue	Gulf Green	Pewter Silver
Midnight Bronze	Sequoia Green	Covert Tan
Mohave Gold	Spring Green	Antique White
Placer Gold	Orange Flame	Cream Yellow
Ascot Blue	Cranberry Red	Golden Brown

Chevrolet

Sport Coupe / Rally Sport / SS / Z28

*Playing further on the theme "closest thing to a 'Vette"
Camaro's approach was almost that of a competitor rather
than a sister division. Comparing the car favorably in many
details, Camaro's major claim for superiority was the additional two rear seats. So far as comparative driving response
and cornering is concerned, Camaro claimed correctly that
it was a true "sports car".*

*Four models were offered, all of them basically the Sport
Coupe. These, in addition to he basic car, were the Rally
Sport, the SS, and the Z28.*

*All continued to feature standard items such as seat belts
plus shoulder belts for the front seats, energy-absorbing
steering columns, seat back latches, padded instrument
panels and sun visors, side-guard beams, cargo-guard luggage
compartment, full roof inner panel, side marker lights,
parking lights that illuminate with the headlights, four-way
hazard warning flasher, back up lights, windshield defroster, washers, and dual-speed wipers, inside and outside rear
view mirror, dual master brake cylinder with warning lights,
and ignition key anti-theft warning.*

*In addition, the RS included a special black grille with ar-
gent accents and a smaller grid pattern, parking lights between the headlights, two-piece split front bumper, dent-
resistant hard rubber grille frame, Rally Sport nameplate on
the fender flanks, and concealed windshield wipers.*

*The SS offered the 200 hp Turbo-Fire 350 V8 as stan-
dard with a 240 hp 396 Turbo-Jet V8 available Option.
Both had chromed air cleaner and heavy-duty starters and
the bigger engine came with standard black-painted rear
body panel. Hide-A-Way wipers and a black grille were part*

Camaro Power Teams

STANDARD				
Engine	SAE net horsepower	Carburetion	Transmission	Rear axle ratio*
Turbo-Thrift 250 250-cu.-in. Six	110	Single-barrel	3-Speed (2.85:1 low) Powerglide	3.08
Turbo-Fire 307 307-cu.-in. V8	130	Two-barrel	3-Speed (2.85:1 low) Powerglide	3.08
			Turbo Hydra-matic	2.73†
AVAILABLE				
Turbo-Fire 350 350-cu.-in. V8	165	Two-barrel	3-Speed (2.54:1 low)# 4-Speed (2.54:1 low)	3.08
			Turbo Hydra-matic	2.73†
Turbo-Fire 350 350-cu.-in. V8 (SS only)	200	Four-barrel	4-Speed (2.54:1 low)	3.42
			Turbo Hydra-matic	3.08
Turbo-Fire 350 350-cu.-in. V8 (Z28 only)	255	Four-barrel	4-Speed (2.52:1 low) 4-Speed (2.20:1 low) Heavy-Duty 4-Speed (2.20:1 low) Turbo Hydra-matic	3.73**
Turbo-Jet 396†† 402-cu.-in. V8 (SS only)	240	Special Four-barrel	4-Speed (2.52:1 low) 4-Speed (2.20:1 low) Turbo Hydra-matic	3.42

*Positraction required for 3.73 and 410
 ratios. Available for all others.
**4.10 performance ratio available.
†3.42 trailering ratio available.
†Not available in California.
#This power team available only with
 California emission system.

For 1972, all Camaro engines have been designed to operate
efficiently on the new low-lead or no-lead gasolines. In addition to the
lower exhaust pollutants attainable with this engine/fuel combination,
there are benefits in longer life for your spark plugs, exhaust system
and other engine components. If these no-lead, low-lead gasolines
are not available, any leaded regular grade gasoline with a research
octane number of 91 or higher may be used.

*of the package as were the 14 x 7 wheels and
F70 x 14 white lettered wide-oval tires. Front
and rear spoilers were standard as was the dual
exhaust and SS fender emblems. With the larger
engine option came a heavier duty front suspension, front and rear stabilizer bars, and special
shock absorbers.*

*The Z28 included the black grille with Z28
emblem, special front stabilizer and shocks,
heavy-duty clutch, power brakes, Positraction,
Z28 fender flank emblems, rear stabilizer bar,
remote controlled sports styled mirror and
matching right-hand mirror, special instrumentation, rally stripes, 15 x 7 wheels and F60 x
15 white lettered tires, and the Turbo-Fire 350
V8 rated at 255 hp. A new 4-speed shifter incorporating a reverse lock-out was an alternate
to the Turbo Hydra-matic transmission.*

1972

The all-vinyl Standard Interior is available in black, blue, green, tan, covert, or white. Doors and sidewalls in matching vinyl, and the doors this year have new map pockets and change receptacles.

The Interior Accent Group includes simulated wood-grained accents on steering wheel and instrument cluster. An Option with Standard Interior, it is included with the Custom Interior Option.

The Custom Interior includes cloth-and-vinyl in black, black/blue, black/green, or black/covert. Also special vinyl door panels with simulated wood-grainted accents, glove compartment light, interior accents as above, special body and hood insulation, and luggage compartment mat.

1972 Camaro Sport Coupe   *Mr. William Valdez, Vista, California*

A new four-spoke steering wheel made its appearance in 1972.

A new "Wet Look" Vinyl Top Option was offered in 1972.

Hood is unchanged.

Standard windshield wipers were visible; Hide-A-Way wipers were included with RS and SS options.

Standard grill has argent-painted grid accent.

Camaro script appears on fender flanks unless SS or Rally Sport is optioned.

Full-width rear bumper dips below license plate behind which fuel filler cap is located.

Side marker lights continue. Lenses differ on right and left sides of car and are accordingly marked.

License plate is recessed into body, illuminated by light above. Luggage compartment lock can be seen just above license plate.

Major standard instruments are speedometer and fuel gauge; tachometer replaces fuel gauge in Special Instrumentation Group; Speedometer maximum reading has been reduced to 130 mph from earlier 150 mph (page 242).

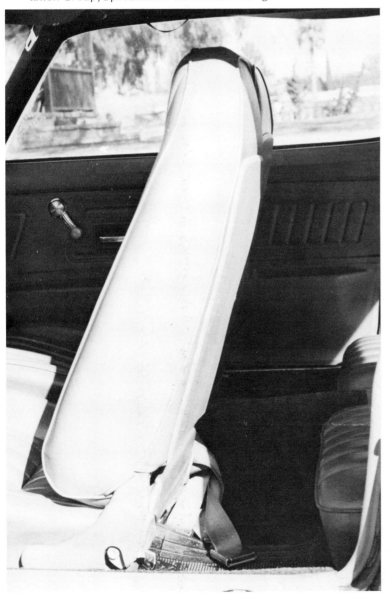

Although not visible in this view, front seats are provided with both seat belts and also shoulder belts.

Upholstery of the two rear seats continues to resemble dual bucket seats.

1973 CAMARO
Building a better way to see the U.S.A.

1973 exterior colors were:

Light Blue Metallic	*Light Green Metallic*
Dark Blue Metallic	*Dark Green Metallic*
Midnight Blue Metallic	*Midnight Green*
Dark Brown Metallic	*Medium Orange Metallic*
Chamois	*Medium Red*
Light Copper Metallic	*Dark Red Metallic*
Green-Gold Metallic	*Silver Metallic*
Light Yellow	*Antique White*

TYPE LT/Z 28/RALLY SPORT/SPORT COUPE   Chevrolet

258

The SS Option had been dropped, but in addition to the basic Sport Coupe, the Rally Sport, and the Z28, a new model was introduced this year. Named the "Type LT", Chevrolet explained that the "L" was for luxury, the "T" for touring. This new model was intended for those who enjoyed both luxury in their travel as well as the handling and feel of a sports car. With standard Turbo Fire 350 2V engine and variable ratio power steering, it had such additional standard items as matched outside rear view mirrors (driver's side remote), Hide-A-Way wipers, black body sills, 14 x 7 Rally Wheels with trim rings and caps, and special LT identification on front, rear quarter and rear end panel. Its interior was luxurious, featuring special trims, and standard Interior Decor/ Sound Group (optional on other models) which included sound deadeners to further quiet the interior. Interior woodgrain vinyl trim was standard as well.

All models had a new front bumper with stronger mounting and front bumper guards (except Rally Sport). The Rally Sport package included a special black grille with silver accents, surrounded by a resilient frame and small side bumperettes. Parking lights appear between the headlamps again, and Hide-A-Way wipers are standard. The Rally Sport name appeared on the fender flanks. The package coud be ordered with the standard Camaro, the Z28, or the new Type LT.

The Z28 option included the Turbo-Fire Special 350 4V V8 engine now rated at 245 horsepower. Operating on regular or no-lead gasoline, it had an open-element air cleaner and hydraulic lifters. For the first time, air conditioning was an available Option on the Z28. Special suspension and F60 x 15 tires on special 15" wheels, power brakes, Positraction, black-finish grille, dual sport mirrors, and Z28 identifications were also included. The familiar stripe pattern was an Option, limited to the Z28, but almost always specified.

Power Teams

	Transmissions		
Standard Engines*	3-Speed	4-Speed	Turbo Hydra-matic
100-hp Turbo-Thrift 250 Six	Std.	—	Avail.
115-hp Turbo-Fire 307 V8	Std.	—	Avail.
Available Engines*			
145-hp Turbo-Fire 350-2 V8**	Std.	Avail.	Avail.
175-hp Turbo-Fire 350-4 V8	Std.	Avail.	Avail.
245-hp Turbo-Fire Special 350-4 V8†	—	Avail.‡	Avail.

*Horsepowers shown are SAE net (as installed) ratings. **Standard engine with Type LT. †Z28 only. ‡Close ratio also available (except with air conditioning).

1973

In addition to upgraded engines and transmissions, the following Options were available:

Four-Season Air conditioning	AM Radio
Tinted glass	AM-FM Radio
Power Steering, Brakes	Rear Seat Speaker
Interior Decor/Quiet Sound Group	Vinyl Roof Cover
Special Instrumentation	Front & Rear Spoilers
Electric Clock (std. on Type LT)	Sport Suspension
Comfortilt Steering Wheel	Heavy-Duty Battery, Radiator
Adjustable Driver's Seat Back	Sport Mirrors
Rear Window Defogger	Hide-A-Way wipers (included on
Visor Vanity Mirror	Rally Sport and Type LT)
Auxiliary Lighting Group	Wheel Covers
Door Edge Guards	Turbine Wheels
Body Side Moldings	Rally Wheels
Accent Carpeting	White stripe or White-lettered tires
Custom Seat Belts	Space Saver Tire

Chevrolet-approved Options available at Dealers:

Audio alarm system	Rear deck luggage carrier
Battery warmer	Luggage compartment light
Locking gas cap	AM/FM Stereo radio
Compass	AM or AM/FM radio with Tape
Fire extinguisher	CB radio
Door edge guards	Spotlight
Trailer wiring harness	Infant safety seat
Trailer hitch	Tissue dispenser
Highway emergency kit	

Rally Sport front end has distinctinve split bumper and more prominent grille.

1973 Rally Sport

Mr. Jim Haines, Santee, California

Hood remains unchanged.

Hide-A-Way windshield wipers are standard on the Rally Sport and Type LT, optional on others.

Body side guards *are* an available Option, but paint striping is a customizing effort.

Rally Sport's parking lights are now clear, not amber. A bright metal trim is available as part of Style Trim Option.

Although an available Option allows for seat back adjustment on driver's side, none is offered for the passenger's seat.

Sports Styled mirrors were an Option; chromed rectangular mirror on left side only was standard.

Optional Vinyl Roof Cover was available in black or white with any exterior color; blue, chamois, green, neutral, or red depending on body color.

Air Spoiler Equipment Option included both front and rear spoilers, available on all models.

Rear spoiler is three-piece; sides curl down over fenders.

Type LT insignia appears on rear panel of those cars.

Ammeter is part of Special Instrumentation Group along with temperature gauge and tachometer.

4-speed shift knob replaced black ball (page 243) in 1971.

New automatic transmission shift knob replaces stirrup type used previously (page 243).

Wood-grained panels on door are standard on new Type LT.

130 mph speedometer is continued; tachometer is part of Special Instrumentation Group Option which is standard on Type LT.

'74 CAMARO

1974 exterior colors are:
Cream Beige
Bright Blue Metallic
Midnight Blue Metallic
Aqua Blue Metallic
Sandstone
Bronze Metallic
Gold Brown Metallic
Lime Yellow

Light Gold Metallic
Medium Red
Bright Green Metallic
Medium Dark Green Metallic
Medium Red Metallic
Silver Metallic
Antique White
Bright Yellow

Building a better way to see the U.S.A. Chevrolet

264

The line-up for 1974 omitted the Rally Sport which was no longer offered. The basic Camaro Sport Coupe was available as is, or it could be Optioned as a Type LT or a Z28, or both, making up to four possible combinations. New heavy case aluminum bumpers and new taillights which wrapped around the sides eliminating the rear marker lights were obvious changes.

The standard V8 in the Sport Coupe was the 350 cu. in. V8 rated at 145 horsepower. Optional versions offered up to 185 hp as power capability continued to slide.

The Type LT interiors continued to present luxury as a selling point. Three mixed-tone cloth-and-vinyl combinations (black/white, black/blue, or green/black) and two all-vinyl combinations (black or neutral) were available. Color-keyed carpeting was standard with red or blue accenting carpet an available Option. Type LT was equipped with the Interior Decor/Quiet Sound Option which was extra on other models. With this, a series of sound deadeners quieted the interior greatly, and special wood-grained accents and bright trim dressed the interior. The Special Instrumentation group, including tachometer and gauges is standard, as are the Hide-A-Way windshield wipers and black-accented body side moldings.

With Camaro, you can be practical. Or go bananas.

Building a better way to see the U.S.A. Chevrolet

POWER TEAMS

Engines	Power Rating*	Carb./ Exh.**	3-Speed	4-Speed	Turbo Hydra-matic
Camaro Sport Coupe:					
Turbo-Thrift 250 Six. Std. (1)	100	1/SE	Std.	Not Avail.	Avail.
Turbo-Fire 350-2 V8. Std. (2)	145	2/SE	Std.	Avail.	Avail.
Turbo-Fire 350-4 V8. Avail. (3, 4)	160	4/SE	Std.	Avail.	Avail.
Turbo-Fire 350-4 V8. Avail. (1, 4)	185	4/DE	Std.	Avail.	Avail.
Type LT Coupe:					
Turbo-Fire 350-2 V8. Std. (2)	145	2/SE	Std.	Avail.	Avail.
Turbo-Fire 350-4 V8. Avail. (3, 4)	160	4/SE	Std.	Avail.	Avail.
Turbo-Fire 350-4 V8. Avail. (1, 4)	185	4/DE	Std.	Avail.	Avail.
Z28 Model Option:					
Turbo-Fire Special 350-4 V8. Avail. (1)	245	4/DE	—	Avail. (5)	Avail.

*The horsepowers shown here are SAE net (as installed) ratings.
**First number indicates number of carburetor barrels, followed by letters for Single Exhaust or Dual Exhaust.
(1) California Emission Equipment required in State of California.
(2) Not available in California.
(3) Available only when California Emission Equipment is ordered.
(4) Available only with power brakes.
(5) Close-Ratio 4-Speed (RPO M21) also available except with air conditioning.

All 1974 Camaro engines are equipped with advanced exhaust emission control systems, and are designed to operate efficiently on unleaded or low-lead fuels of at least 91 Research Octane. In addition to the lower exhaust emissions attainable, there are benefits in longer life for your spark plugs, exhaust system and other engine components. If these unleaded, low-leaded gasolines are not available, any leaded 91 Research Octane or higher regular grade fuel containing 0.5 grams, or less, of lead per gallon should be used.

Camaro vital statistics: Wheelbase—108". Overall length—195.4". Height loaded—49.1". Front tread—61.3". Rear tread—60.0". Front head room—37.3". Rear head room—36.0". Front hip room—56.7". Rear hip room—47.3". Front shoulder room—56.7". Rear shoulder room—54.4". Front leg room—43.9". Rear leg room—29.6".

The Z28 option has as standard engine the 350 V8 4V dual exhaust version rated at 245 hp and featuring a new air cleaner with dual air intake tubes and chromed cover. Also standard are ribbed aluminum valve covers. The Z28 option features a special sports suspension, wide 15 x 7 wheels with center caps and trim rings, and wide oval F60-15 bias belted white-lettered tires. Also a heavy-duty starter, and radiator, power brakes, Positraction rear axle and both right and left side sports styled rear view mirrors. Front and rear spoilers as well as the distinctive stripes were Options.

Power windows had again become an available Option, other options were as offered in 1973 (page 260).

1974 Camaro Z28

1974 Camaro Sport Coupe   *Mrs. Rose Pate, Carlsbad, California*

Mr. Alfredo Garcia, Oceanside, California

1974

Standard grill is painted silver.

Z28 grill is black-painted.

Headlights are now deeply recessed in forward-sweeping fenders.

Parking lights are also deeply recessed and have attractive trim strip.

New bright anodized aluminum full-width bumpers with black rubber impact strips replace the pressed steel earlier types.

Familiar Z28 insignia no longer appears on front grille.

Camaro grille insignia appears on all models, Z28 included.

268

Appearance of the hood is greatly changed by the addition of the optional Z28 hood stripes.

Type LT insignia appears on the roof rear quarter when applicable.

Sport Coupe rear roof quarter is unadorned.

Z28 graphics are outstanding. Motif is also repeated on optional rear spoiler.

Z28 graphics extend over optional rear spoiler. Dual exhaust system is standard for this model.

Standard rear end slopes to rear panel without uplifing effect of optional rear spoiler.

New for 1974 are the wrap-around taillights also replacing the former rear side markers (page 262).

Model year information is again molded into taillight lenses.

New full-width bright anodized aluminum bumpers add weight to the appearance of rear end (Compare page 262).

Script Camaro will appear on rear panel unless replaced with "Type LT" when applicable.

Standard instruments are a 130 mph speedometer and a matching fuel gauge. Also warning lights for temperature, oil pressure, and ammeter.

Special Instrumentation Group also provides 130 mph speedometer but substitutes a tachometer and instruments to replace standard warning lights.

A console trim plate improves appearance of floor shifter.

The standard 4-spoke steering wheel bears a legend at its hub either the Camaro insignia (right) or an LT or Z28 button.

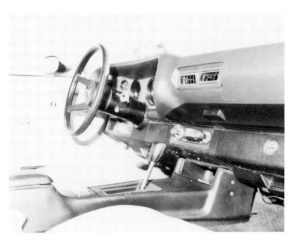

In addition to AM radio, AM-FM, or AM-FM stereo, a Dealer Option included an AM-FM Stereo with tape.

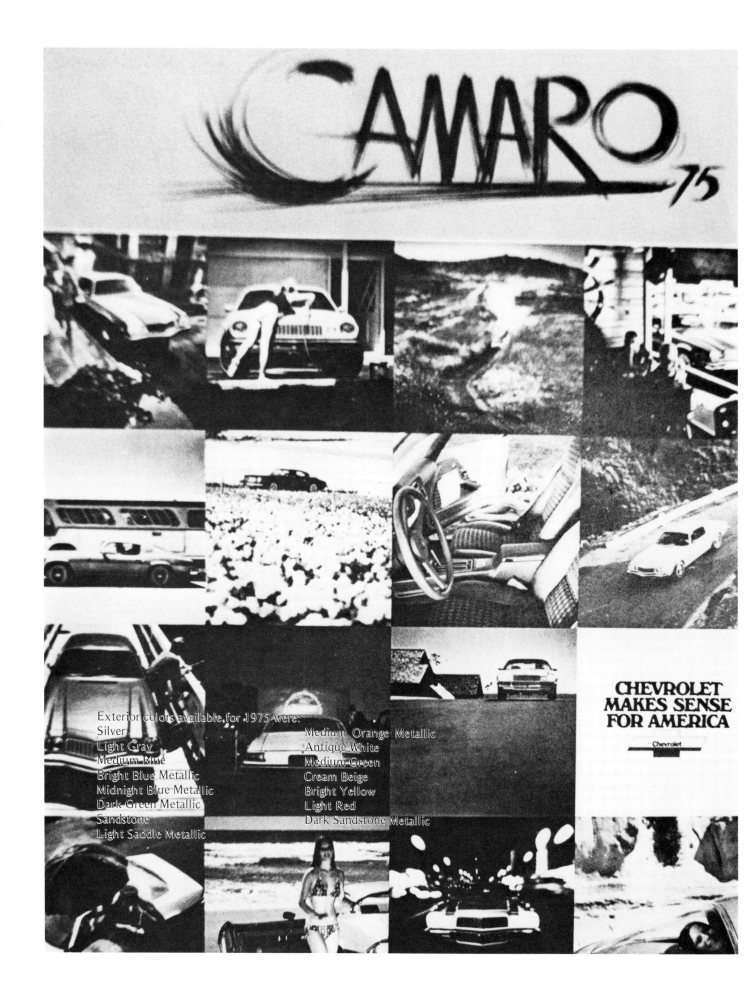

CAMARO 75

Exterior colors available for 1975 were:
Silver
Light Gray
Medium Blue
Bright Blue Metallic
Midnight Blue Metallic
Dark Green Metallic
Sandstone
Light Saddle Metallic

Medium Orange Metallic
Antique White
Medium Green
Cream Beige
Bright Yellow
Light Red
Dark Sandstone Metallic

**CHEVROLET
MAKES SENSE
FOR AMERICA**

Chevrolet

The Z28 was dropped from the 1975 line, a victim of rising insurance rates, continuing and additional government standards, and a public perception of the car as a fuel-hungry machine in an age of Arab-imposed fuel shortage. Starting the year with just two models, the Sport Coupe and the Type LT, Chevrolet presented the Camaro as either "the lower priced Sport Coupe" or "the luxurious Type LT".

The Sport Coupe had all of the standard features of Camaro, including a floor-mounted 3-speed transmission, inner fender liners, 4-spoke sport steering wheel, steel guard beams in the doors, front disc brakes, coolant recovery system, power steering, double-panel steel roof, doors, and deck lid, and a perforated acoustical headlining to reduce sound. A transistorized High Energy Ignition (HEI) system eliminated the points and condenser, a Catalytic converter reduced exhaust emissions, and all engines ran on unleaded fuel. Interiors were black, saddle, or sandstone vinyl and a choice of black or sandstone cloth with vinyl was also available.

Type LT was offered as a step up from the basic Sport Coupe. It featured birds-eye maple simulated wood-grain on the instrument panel which included the tachometer and display instruments of the Special Instrumentation Package. The 350 cu. in. V8 engine was standard; seats were more deeply contoured, and trimmed in knit cloth or vinyl; for the first time a full-leather interior in dark red or saddle was also available. Sport mirrors on both sides were included as were exterior trim items on the parking lamps and the Hide-A-Way windshield wipers. Type LT emblems appeared on the rear roof quarters and rear panel, and Rally wheels with center caps and trim rings were standard.

In Janaury of 1975, Chevrolet re-introduced the Camaro Rally Sport which was truly an unusual re-styling. Featuring a black hood, grille, front and rear panel, headlamp bezel, and roof, this upper section was outlined with a three-color stripe adding to the impact. Also featured was the rally sport identification on the front fender flanks, dual black sport mirrors, and FR78-14 white-lettered pension including rear stabilizer and heavy duty front stabilizer and shock absorbers were also available. A Gymkhana Suspension Package included the special suspension plus E60-15 tires on 15 x 7 styled wheels which were painted body color and furnished with a trim ring and small hub cap.

Engines

Type	Disp.	Horse-power	Carb. Barrels	Exhaust	Model
Six (1)	250	105	1	Sgl.	Sport Coupe
V8 (2)	350	145	2	Sgl.*	Both
V8 (1)	350	155	4	Sgl.*	Both

*With dual tail pipes.
(1) California Emission Equipment required in California.
(2) Not available in California.

1975

Some addition Options were:
- *Console*
- *Turbine wheels*
- *Space Saver Tire*
- *Power door locks*
- *Padded vinyl roof cover*
- *Body side moldings*
- *Power windows*
- *Front and rear spoilers*
- *Special Instrumentation*
- *Adjustable driver's seat back*
- *Style Trim Group*
- *Rear window defogger*
- *AM, AM/FM, or AM/FM Stereo*
- *Rear seat speaker*
- *Dual horns*
- *Sports Decor Group*
- *Interior Decor Group*
- *Comfortilt steering wheel*
- *Door edge guards*
- *Tinted glass*
- *Air conditioning*
- *Etc.*

Bumpers are cast bright-anodized aluminum with integral hard rubber rub strips.

1975 Camaro Sport Coupe *Mr. Robert Godinez, National City, California*

New wrap-around rear window greatly improves rearward visibility (compare page 270).

Camaro identification emblem appears on fender flanks of Sport Coupe and Type LT, but is replaced with Rally sport *decal* with that option.

Windshield wipers on the Sport Coupe are not concealed. Those on Type LT and Rally Sport are.

Optional rear spoiler adds visual framing of rear light when viewed from the side.

Taillights are protected by bumper wrapped around corner.

The license plate recess is painted body color except on Rally Sport which also, features black-painted rear panel.

The major effect of the optional rear spoiler is to improve appearance of rear of the car; its actual running effect is questionable.

New inner circle of graduations on the speedometer mark kilometers per mile and are in addition to continuing 130 mph indication. Fuel gauge is now lettered with admonition to use "unleaded gas only". Panel behind the instruments is covered with birds-eye maple vinyl grain on Type LT.

Standard steering wheel is four-spoke introduced in 1972; horn button is replaced with LT as appropriate.

Power teams.

Engine	Net HP Rating	Engine* Usage	3-Speed Manual	4-Speed Manual	Turbo Hydra-matic
250 1-bbl. Six (4.1 Litre)	105	Std. N.A. for LT	Std.**	N.A.	Avail.
305 2-bbl. V8 (5.0 Litre)	140	Std.	Std.**	N.A.	Avail.
350 4-bbl. V8 (5.7 Litre)	165	Avail.	N.A.	Avail.**	Avail.

*California Emission Equipment required in California.   **Not available in California.   N.A.—Not Available

Three models were again offered in 1976, the Camaro Sport Coupe, the Type LT, and the Rally Sport. Basically similar to last year's models, some few new variations were, of course, added. The optional Vinyl Sport Roof now ended above the rear window (page 295), and several engineering improvements intended to improve fuel economy, give cleaner exhaust, faster starts and warm-ups, and reduce time between tune-ups, first introduced on the 1975 models, were carried forward. These included the High Energy Ignition (HEI) transistorized ignition, the catalytic converter, a new duct system for carburetor intake air, and Early Fuel Evaporation, a system that uses exhaust gases to pre-heat the incoming fuel/air mixture during warm-up.

Again the cars all featured the long-hood, short-deck styling with wrap around taillights. Magic-Mirror acrylic lacquer exteriors were offered in Light Blue Metallic, Dark Blue Metallic, Firethorn Metallic, Mahogany Metallic, Lime Green Metallic, Dark Green Metallic, Buckskin, Cream, Bright Yellow, Medium Orange Metallic, Medium Saddle Metallic, Black, Silver, and Antique White.

The Sport Coupe was provided with a new bright metal lower rocker panel molding (also included with the Type LT option) and a single outside rearview mirror was standard.

The Type LT Coupe had Hide-A-Way wipers, dual outside sport rear view mirrors, 14 x 7" Rally wheels, brushed-finish rear panel, and the Special Instrumentation package. The steering wheel, column, and lower instrumentation panel was color-keyed, and deep-contour bucket seats were included.

Rally Sport's package included black finished hood, roof, rocker and rear end panels, and grille. Also tri-color striping and rally sport decal on fenders along with 14 inch Rally wheels, argent painted.

Other factory Options remained as previously offered, but one newly resurrected Option was the popular Cruise-Master speed control.

1976 Camaro

CHEVROLET

Type LT has special hornbutton insert on steering wheel
in addition to other features.

1976 Camaro Type LT

Miss Deen Austin, Solana Beach, California

1976

The distinctive Camaro emblem appears again on the front header panel.

This view of car in unchanged from previous (page 274).

Side marker light lenses are not interchangeable from left to right side.

Dual outside rear view mirrors are standard on the Type LT with driver's side remote controlled.

Vertical trim on parking lights is part of available Style Trim Group.

Hide-A-Way wipers are standard on Type LT; recessed behind hood they are not visible from the front.

Vehicle's identification number continues to be embossed into the instrument panel.

Camaro insignia appears on fender flanks (except rally sport).

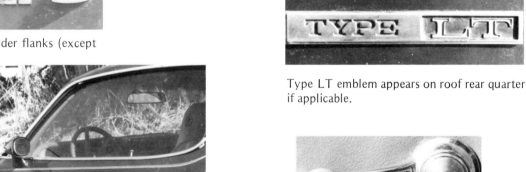

Type LT emblem appears on roof rear quarter if applicable.

Rocker panel molding appears at bottom of doors, Sport Coupe and Type LT.

Inside door latch handles are recessed for safety.

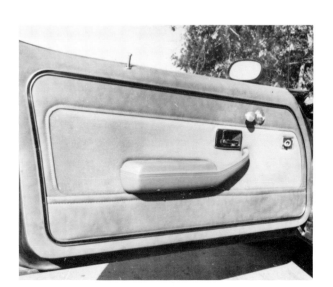

Type LT doors have molded arm rest with integral door pull.

The wider rear window, introduced on 1975 models, is clearly an improvement over earlier style (page 255.)

Rear deck lid latch is released by lock above license plate.

Type LT only has a brushed-finish rear panel. Sport Coupe panel is body color, Rally Sport is painted black.

A reminder to use unleaded fuel only is made by a decal placed below license plate.

Back up light lens is inset into the wraparound taillight lens.

Position of the optional Comfortilt steering wheel is secured by lever under turn signal arm.

The pushbutton automatic transmission shift knob introduced in 1973, continues.

Standard windshield wiper/ washer is controlled by switch on panel below light switch.

A seat belt reminder light and warning buzzer became standard in 1975.

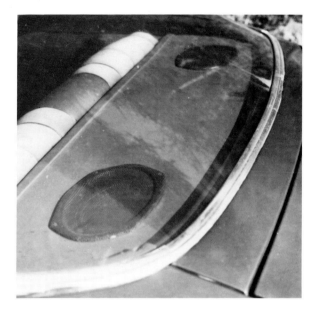

The two rear speakers for optional AM/FM stereo radio are recessed in rear package shelf.

AM/FM radio has dual dial scale with sliding bar selector. Similar AM/FM stereo tape unit has dial which pivots to accept tape cartridge.

'77 Camaro

Exterior colors for 1977:
Light Blue Metallic
Dark Blue Metallic
Aqua Metallic
Medium Green Metallic
Light Buckskin
Brown Metallic
  (all above new for 1977)

Silver
Black
Firethorn Metallic
Bright Yellow
Light Red
Orange Metallic

POWER TEAMS

Engine	Power Rating*	Engine Usage	3-Speed Manual Standard (1)	4-Speed Manual Available (1)	Turbo Hydra-matic Available (2)
250-1 barrel Six	110	Standard	2.73† Standard 3.08† Avail. (3)	NA	2.73† Standard 3.08† Avail. (3,4)
305-2 barrel V8	145	Avail. (5,6)	2.73†	NA	2.56†
350-4 barrel V8	170	Avail. (6)	NA	3.08†	2.56† Standard 3.08† Avail. (3,4)

*SAE net (as installed) rating. NA—Not Available. †Axle ratio.
SPECIAL NOTE: California Emission Equipment required for registration in California. In other states, High Altitude Emission Equipment may be required in areas 4,000 feet or more above sea level.
(1) Not available in California or with High Altitude Emission Equipment.
(2) Required in California and with High Altitude Emission Equipment.
(3) Performance ratio.
(4) Included with High Altitude Emission Equipment.
(5) Not available with High Altitude Emission Equipment.
(6) Power brakes required with V8 engines.

Commencing the year with two models, the Sport Coupe and the Type LT, and a Rally Sport option available on either, on February 18, 1977 at the International Race Of Champions (IROC) finale at Dayona, Chevrolet re-introduced the popular Z28.

All models had the distincitve long-hood, short-rear deck styling, and all had Hide-A-Way wipers. Also standard were wraparound taillights, aluminum bumpers with protective black rubber strips, bright lower moldings, windshield and rear window moldings, contoured bucket seats, 4-spoke steering wheel, built-in hearter-defroster system, and a flow-through ventilation that started when ignition was switched on. Front disc brakes, variable-ratio power steering were also standard.

The Type LT included sport mirrors, dual horns, Rally wheels with bright center caps and trim rings, special instrumentation, the Interior Decor/Quiet Sound Group, bright grille outline molding, a black-finished accent panel below the lower body molding, a bright-aluminum rear trim panel, Type LT nameplates on the roof rear quarters and steering wheel, bright trim rings and center bar on the parking lights, and inside, the special Type LT deep contour bucket seats. Its instrument panel had a simulated leather cluster facing, and a color-coordinated four-spoke steering wheel.

The new Z28 came with black-out grille, body-colored bumpers, body-colored 15 x 7 special wheels with white-lettered G70 steel belted radial tires, dual exhaust, double sports mirrors, new "string-wrapped" steering wheel, tachometer and gauges, power front disc brakes, front and rear spoilers (now no longer an Option), special sports suspension, stowaway spare tire, "Z28" identifications on front, sides, and back, and a standard 350 cu. in. 4V V8 with heavy-duty rear axle and standard 4-speed manual transmission (Turbo Hydra-matic required in California).

The Rally Sport package. available on either the Sport Coupe or the Type LT included, as before, contrasting paint areas on forward portions of the roof, rear end panel and license opening, around side windows, upper portion of doors, top surface of fenders, hood and header panel. Previously available only in black, these areas were offered in grey metallic, blue metallic, or buckskin metallic for 1977, all with harmonizing tri-color accent stripe. The package also included bright trim on the headlights, Rally wheels, and rally sport decals on the fenders and deck lid.

Available Options were virtually unchanged, but a new addition to the list was a T-top with removable panels.

1977 Camaro Z28

Weseloh Chevrolet, Carlsbad, California

Appearance of front end does not differ substantially from 1976.

Camaro emblem again appears on the front header panel of all models.

Replacable front cap is styled to blend into fenders.

Front bumper guards are an Option that was introduced in 1976.

Plain hood was for the Sport Coupe and the Type LT.

The newly styled Z28 decal appears on the fender flanks in addition to the standard Camaro insignia which is used with all except Rally Sport optioned models.

Highly distinctive new hood for the Z28 becomes an obvious identification aid.

1977

Wrap around taillights are trimmed with bright-metal moldings.

The new Z28 decal appears above the rear panel on the spoiler.

Front and rear spoilers are standard equipment on the 1977 Z28.

Rear lights are black-outlined on Z28 only.

Special identifications are placed on the steering wheel hub (below) and the door (right).

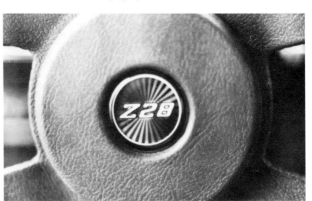

A new Option became available during 1977. The T-top is a psuedo-Convertible with two removable roof panels providing an open-air feeling similar to that of the folding roof Convertible.

Latches secure the four corners of each panel.

Panels and lip of opening are trimmed in bright metal.

Removable glass roof panels are tinted.

When removed, the panels leave a solid center section in the roof; hence the T-top appellation.

1978 CAMARO

Chevrolet

Exterior colors available for 1978 were:

Bright Blue Metallic

Dark Blue-Green Metallic

Camel Metallic

Saffron Metallic

Dark Camel Metallic

Carmine Metallic
  (all new for 1978)

Also:

White

Silver

Black

Light Blue

Bright Yellow

Light Red

Again the Sport Coupe, the Type LT, and the Z28 were offered, and the Rally Sport option was available with the first two. All Camaros featured a newly styled urethane front end with new grille, and similar new rear appearance. A new Delco Freedom battery was sealed to eliminate servicing; and new color-keyed aluminum wheels became an available Option. All cars continued the standard SIX with the V8 standard only on the Z28. Other standard features included 3-speed manual transmission (4-speed on Z28), power steering, front disc brakes, audible wear sensors in the brake linings, bucket seats, center dome light, day/ night rear view mirror, color-keyed steering column and steering wheel. All had catalytic converters and radial tires, Hide-A-Way wipers and flow-though ventilation. All models featured both front and rear stabilizer bars as standard equipment.

The Type LT featured its special deep-contour front bucket seats, the Interior Decor/Sound Quiet package, the Special Instrumentation package, color-keyed Rally wheels with bright center caps and trim rings, bright grille and outline moldings, and dual sport mirrors and dual horns.

The Rally Sport added the familiar black-finish hood and roof with tri-color trim stripe, rear spoiler, black-finished grille and headlight bezels and dual sport mirrors.

The Z28 featured the 350 cu. in. V8 with a four barrel carburetor, standard 4-speed transmission (Turbo Hydra-matic only in California), dual exhaust, GR70-15 wide tires on 7" special Z28 body-colored wheels, and a special Sport suspension. Also featured were the Special Instrumentation Group, a space-saving Stowaway tire, rear spoiler, dual mirrors, black finished grille and window moldings, and front fender louvers.

Some of the more popular Options were a Power Door Lock system, Rear window defogger, Comfortilt steering wheel, AM, AM/FM stereo or monaural radio. AM- or AM/FM stereo radio with 8-track tape, center console, Vinyl Sport Roof, rear spoiler, Cruise-Master speed control, etc. Additional other options were unchanged from previous.

1978 Camaro power teams: All States Except California

Engines	Power Rating†	Type LT & Sport Coupe	Z28	3-Speed Manual (STD.)	4-Speed Manual	4-Speed Close-Ratio Manual††	Automatic Below 4,000 Ft.	4,000 Ft. and Above
250 Cu. In. L6	110	STD.	NA	2.73	NA	NA	2.73	NA
305 Cu. In. V8	145	AVAIL.	NA	NA	3.08	NA	2.41	NA
350 Cu. In. V8	170/160▲	AVAIL.	STD.	NA	3.08	3.73	2.41*/3.42**	3.08/3.42**

California Only

250 Cu. In. L6	90	STD.	NA	NA	NA	NA	2.73	NA
305 Cu. In. V8	135	AVAIL.	NA	NA	NA	NA	2.41	NA
350 Cu. In. V8	160	AVAIL.	STD.	NA	NA	NA	2.41*/3.42**	NA

†S.A.E. net horsepower as installed. *3.08 Performance Ratio available. **Z28 only.
▲Rating with High Altitude Emission Equipment. ††4-Speed Close-Ratio Manual Z28 only.
STD.—Standard. NA—Not Available.

SPECIAL NOTE: California Emission Equipment required for registration in California. In other states, High Altitude Emission Equipment may be required in areas 4,000 feet or more above sea level.

1978

1978 Camaro Type LT

Type LT emblem appears on rear roof quarters.

Mrs. Jo Miller, Oceanside, California

Type LT insignia appears on grille of that model which also features bright grille and outline moldings.

New urethane front end cap is resilient, and features body-colored front bumper system.

All models have new emblem on grille in place of earlier style on the header panel (page 286).

Integral front bumper is part of one-piece energy-absorbing protective front end extending completely across the car.

Optional Vinyl Roof Cover extends forward across roof from just above back of the windows.

Hide-A-Way wipers are standard on all models for 1978.

New rectangular parking lights replace round ones of 1977 (page 287). Horizontal trim bar is part of the Style Trim Option included with the Type LT.

Bright trim around headlamps is standard on Sport Coupe and Type LT but is black-painted on Rally Sport and Z28.

Color-keyed inserts in door handles are part of the Style Trim Group, an Option included with the Type LT.

Luggage compartment light is part of Auxiliary lighting group which also includes underhood, ashtray, courtesy, and glove compartment lights and headlight reminder buzzer.

The stowaway spare tire and accompanying inflator are standard on the Z28, Option on other models.

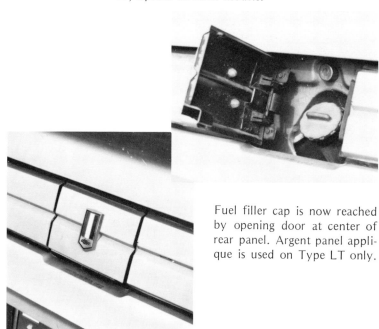

Fuel filler cap is now reached by opening door at center of rear panel. Argent panel applique is used on Type LT only.

New wrap around taillights have separate red, orange, and inner white, lenses.

New energy-absorbing resilient urethane rear bumper system continues body color; license plate now recessed below bumper.

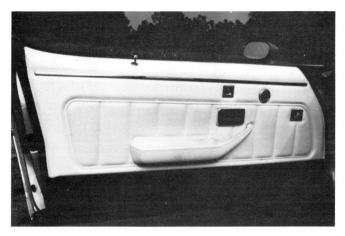

Type LT door panels feature distinctive trim pattern and carpeting on the lower portion.

Power door lock buttons on doors lock both doors.

Power windows are operated by this switch on the mandatory console.

Type LT, Z28, and available on others as Special Instrumentation Group, feature tachometer and indicating gauges.

Type LT insignia appears on the doors and steering wheel hub (lower left).

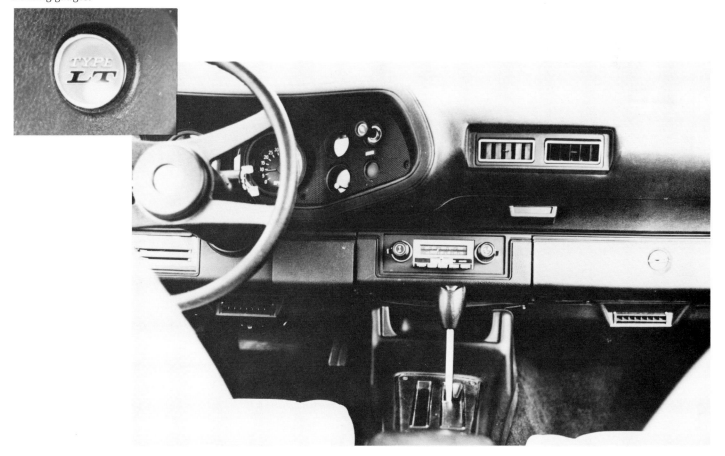

Camaro

Chevrolet

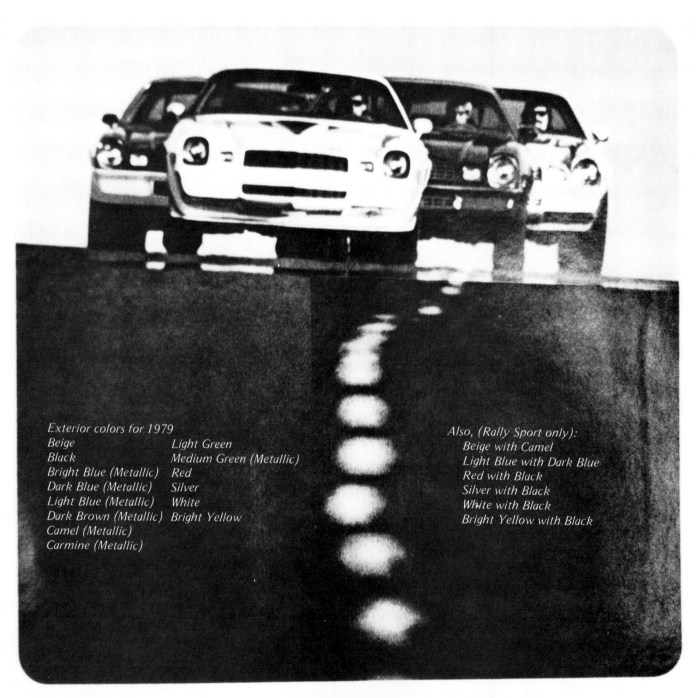

Exterior colors for 1979
Beige	Light Green
Black	Medium Green (Metallic)
Bright Blue (Metallic)	Red
Dark Blue (Metallic)	Silver
Light Blue (Metallic)	White
Dark Brown (Metallic)	Bright Yellow
Camel (Metallic)	
Carmine (Metallic)	

Also, (Rally Sport only):
Beige with Camel
Light Blue with Dark Blue
Red with Black
Silver with Black
White with Black
Bright Yellow with Black

1979

The Type LT was gone, replaced with a newly named model, the Camaro Berlinetta. The Z28, the Rally Sport, and the Sport Coupe were continued.

All cars shared standard features including the Delco Freedom sealed battery; concealed windshield wipers; a coolant recovery system; front disc brakes; front coil and rear leaf springs; power steering; inner fender liners and double-wall construction in doors, roof, and deck lid; High Energy ignition, front stabilizer bar; bucket seats; steel-belted radial tires; flow-through ventilation; and visible ball joint wear indicators. Also standard were bright windshield and rear window moldings (except Z28); four-spoke steering wheel; built-in heater-defroster system; catalytic converter; generator with built-in solid state regulator, etc.

The Rally Sport included the special paint scheme as previously along with special identifications including a decal placed above its fender flank Camaro insignia, sport mirrors, and color-keyed Rally wheels.

The new Berlinetta featured a deluxe insulating package to quiet the interior; tuned engine mounts and revalved shock absorbers; front spring isolators and larger body mounts. Also included were new front bucket seats with a bright-accented instrument panel containing the Special Instrumentation Group of tachometer and gauges. The Berlinetta had a bright-accented grille, dual pin stripes, the custom styled wheels, black-painted rocker panel, and a new Berlinetta emblem on front, rear and roof rear quarters.

The Z28 continued to be presented as Camaro's most aggressive model. Featuring a standard 350 cu. in. (5.7 litre) 4-barrel carburetor V8 engine rated at 175 horsepower (170 in California) and dual exhausts, it was the most powerful offered now. Also on the Z28 were special springs, shocks, and rear stabilizer and a 4-speed manual transmission (except in California where only the automatic transmission was offered). Special 15 x 7 body-color wheels were standard as was the simulated string-wrapped four-spoke steering wheel. Inside there were the expected tachometer and gauges, on the hood was the simulated air induction scoop, and on the fenders were simulated louvers. The rear spoiler was standard too as were the dual sport mirrors, and a new low-slung from air dam joined flared front fenders. Unique Z28 striping completed the package.

Available Options were virtually unchanged. By now the published list had reached 55 separate items, including nine combinations of AM, AM/FM, and tape system sound options alone.

CAMARO POWER TEAMS

Engine	Ordering Code	Power Rating*	Displacement (cubic inches)	Engine Availability		Transmission Availability			
				All Models Except Z28	Z28 Only	Three-Speed Manual (1)	Four-Speed Manual (1)	Four-Speed Close-Ratio Manual (1)	Automatic (2)
ALL STATES EXCEPT CALIFORNIA									
4.1 Litre 1-Bbl. L6 **(A)**	L22	115	250	Std.	NA	Std.	NA	NA	EC
5.0 Litre 2-Bbl. V8 **(B)**	LG3	130	305	EC (3)	NA	NA	EC	NA	EC
5.7 Litre 4-Bbl. V8 **(B)**	LM1	170	350	EC (3)	NA	NA	EC	NA	EC
5.7 Litre 4-Bbl. V8 **(B)**	LM1	175	350	NA	Std.	NA	NA	Std.	EC
ALL STATES EXCEPT CALIFORNIA (with High Altitude Emission Equipment)									
5.7 Litre 4-Bbl. V8 **(B)**	LM1	165	350	EC (3)	NA	NA	NA	NA	EC
CALIFORNIA ONLY (with California Emission Requirements)									
4.1 Litre 1-Bbl. L6 **(A)**	L22	90	250	Std.	NA	NA	NA	NA	EC
5.0 Litre 2-Bbl. V8 **(B)**	LG3	125	305	EC (3)	NA	NA	NA	NA	EC
5.7 Litre 4-Bbl. V8 **(B)**	LM1	165	350	EC (3)	NA	NA	NA	NA	EC
5.7 Litre 4-Bbl. V8 **(B)**	LM1	170	350	NA	Std.	NA	NA	NA	EC

*S.A.E. net horsepower as installed.   Std.—Standard.   NA—Not Available.   EC—Available at extra cost.
(1) With floor-mounted shift control.   (2) Floor console (RPO D55) required.   (3) Power brakes (RPO J50) required.

(A) PRODUCED BY GM—CHEVROLET MOTOR DIVISION.
(B) PRODUCED BY GM—CHEVROLET MOTOR DIVISION AND GM OF CANADA.

1979 Camaro Rally Sport

1979 Camaro Z28

Mr. Ron Goodin, Oceanside, California

Miss Candace Pingree, Orange, California

Other than the Z28, all models feature bright-accented grille and light bezels.

A redesigned emblem (compare page 294) is affixed to the grille on all models.

A new front air dam is standard on the Z28.

Z28 features include the black-painted grill and light bezels.

A new Option, the Electric Rear Window Defogger operates by heating the glass with a grid of imbedded wires.

Rear window moldings, like those on windshield, are black on Z28, bright on others.

Rally Sport decal appears over the standard Camaro emblem which is deleted on Z28.

Simulated louvers are added to front fenders of Z28.

Other models do not have lower spoiler although rear one is an available Option.

The unique Z28 two-color stripe pattern crosses the front of new lower air dam, flares upward, and ends near rear of door with repeat of Z28 identification.

1979

Z28 identification appears on standard rear spoiler.

Rear spoiler is also standard on Rally Sport, and an available Option on others.

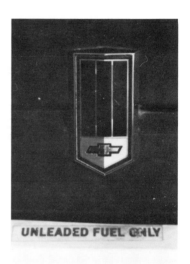

A new emblem also appears on fuel tank filler access door.

Rally Sport and Z28 have similar appearance from the rear. Sport Coupe lacks the standard rear spoiler. Berlinetta has bright-accent molding in horizontal groove on taillight lens assembly.

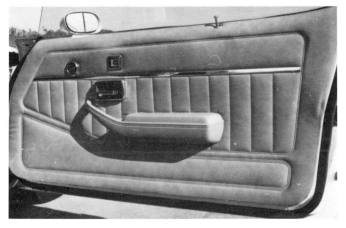

If applicable, a Z28 or Berlinetta identification button appears on the door panel.

Optional Power door lock system places control button on each door.

Standard interior door panel has all-vinyl trim; Custom interior adds carpeting at lower portion.

Special Instrumentation package, standard with Z28, again includes the tachometer and gauges.

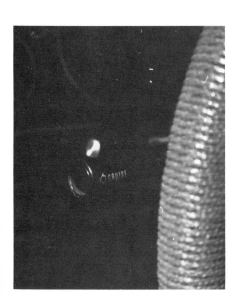

Z28 steering wheel has simulated string-wrapping adding to rim diameter.

Z28 identification appears on horn button.

1979 Z28 Standard Interior.

1980

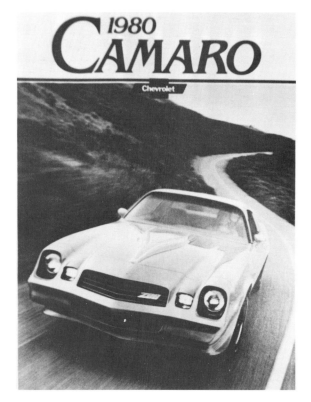

New speedometer for 1980 has mere 85 mph full scale reading; 55 mph indicated in red.

New optional Aluminum Wheels in 15 x 7 for the Z28 or 14 x 7 for the others were introduced; not much else was altered. That Camaro was in <u>need</u> of change was indicated by one major automotive magazine which, regarding the Z28, stated "A medieval warrior on the path to a rocking chair".

CAMARO POWER TEAMS

Engine	Order-ing Code	Power Rating*	Displace-ment (cubic inches)	All Models Except Z28	Z28 Only	Three-Speed Manual (1)	Four-Speed Manual (1)	Auto-matic
				Engine Availability		Transmission Availability		
ALL STATES EXCEPT CALIFORNIA								
3.8 Liter 2-Bbl. V6 (A)	LC3	115	229	Std.	NA	Std.	NA	EC
4.4 Liter 2-Bbl. V8 (B)	L39	120	267	EC(2)	NA	NA	NA	EC
5.0 Liter 4-Bbl. V8 (B)	LG4	155	305	EC(2)	NA	NA	EC	EC
5.7 Liter 4-Bbl. V8 (A)	LM1	190	350	NA	Std.	NA	Std.	EC
CALIFORNIA ONLY (with California Emission Requirements)								
3.8 Liter 2-Bbl. V6 (C)	LD5	110	231	Std.	NA	NA	NA	EC
5.0 Liter 4-Bbl. V8 (B)	LG4	155	305	EC(2)	NA	NA	NA	EC
5.0 Liter 4-Bbl. V8 (B)	LG4	165	305	NA	Std.	NA	NA	EC

*S.A.E. net horsepower as installed. Std.—Standard. NA—Not Available.
EC–Available at extra cost.
(1) With floor-mounted shift control.
(2) Power brakes (RPO J50) required.
(A) PRODUCED BY GM–CHEVROLET MOTOR DIVISION.
(B) PRODUCED BY GM–CHEVROLET MOTOR DIVISION AND GM OF CANADA.
(C) PRODUCED BY GM–BUICK MOTOR DIVISION.

1981

Z28's air induction hood was now functional, and its 4-speed manual shift once again available in California, but little else varied as the end of the model run neared.

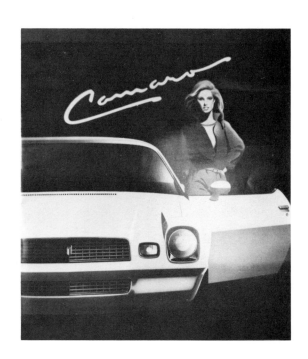

CAMARO POWER TEAMS.

ENGINE	Order-ing Code	Displace-ment (cu. in.)	Sport Coupe & Berlinetta	Z28	3-speed Manual (1)	4-speed Manual (1)	Auto-matic
			Engine Availability		Transmission Availability		
ALL STATES EXCEPT CALIFORNIA							
3.8 Liter 2-Bbl. V6 (A)	LC3	229	Std.	NA	Std.	NA	Opt.
4.4 Liter 2-Bbl. V8 (B)	L39	267	Opt.	NA	NA	NA	Opt.
5.0 Liter 4-Bbl. V8 (B)	LG4	305	Opt.	Std.	NA	Opt. (Std. Z28)	Opt. (NA Z28)
5.7 Liter 4-Bbl. V8 (A)	LM1	350	NA	Opt.	NA	NA	Opt.
CALIFORNIA ONLY							
3.8 Liter 2-Bbl. V6 (C)	LD5	231	Std.	NA	NA	NA	Opt.
5.0 Liter 4-Bbl. V8 (B)	LG4	305	Opt.	Std.	NA	Opt. (Std. Z28)	Opt. (NA Z28)
5.7 Liter 4-Bbl. V8 (A)	LM1	350	NA	Opt.	NA	NA	Opt.

Std.—Standard. NA—Not Available. Opt.—Optional. (1) With floor-mounted shift control.
PRODUCED BY GM: (A) CHEVROLET MOTOR DIVISION. (B) CHEVROLET MOTOR DIVISION; GM OF CANADA. (C) BUICK MOTOR DIVISION.

The four available models, the Sport Coupe, the Rally Sport, the Berlinetta, and the Z28 were continued on for 1980; but the attractive Rally Sport was dropped in 1981. Changes were minimal, and not always obvious, but there were some items altered. In 1981, the 4-speed transmission was again available in California with the Z28, and a new electronic diagnostic system was incorporated in all cars.

The Computer Command Control continuously monitors the car's performance, making constant revisions to the fuel/air mixture. Intended as a device with which the fuel economy might be improved, the CCM also reportedly reduces the exhaust emissions while adjusting for varying conditions of temperature, altitude, and barometric pressure as well. It is also self-diagnostic, and helps pinpoint problems should a malfunction appear.

1981 Camaro Sport Coupe   *Weseloh Chevrolet, Carlsbad, California*

Bright-accented grill is unchanged for 1980-81.

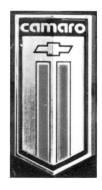

New grille emblem appears for 1980 replacing 1979 item (page 304).

Z28 has grill featuring horizontal bars and Z28 insignia rather than Camaro emblem.

Color inserts in door handles remain part of optional Style Trim Group.

Z28 hood for 1981 has solenoid-operated cold air induction system, but is visually similar to earlier style.

Headlight and parking light bezels of Z28 are black painted (left), those on Sport Coupe and Berlinetta are bright metal.

Sport Coupe and Berlinetta feature bright metal moldings around rear window; Z28 (right) is black-painted.

Taillight lenses are unchanged, but Z28 (right) has black horizontal band.

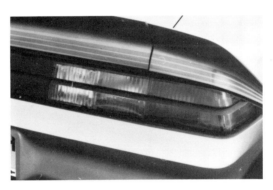

Z28 front fenders have simulated air scoops.

New Camaro emblem is repeated on gas filler access door except on Z28.

Price of a typical 1981 Camaro Sport Coupe has reached over $8600, more than double that of a comparably equipped 1967 model at introduction.

Standard 1967 Hub Cap

Optional 1967 Full Wheel Cover.

1967 14'' Disc Brake wheel, trim ring, and cap; note lettering.

1968 15 x 6 Z28 wheel with original white-lettered Goodyear E70 x 15 tire.

Original 1969 Goodyear F70 x 14 tire and wheel.

1968 Z28 15 x 6 Rally wheel with cap and trim ring. Note cap lettering differs from 1967.

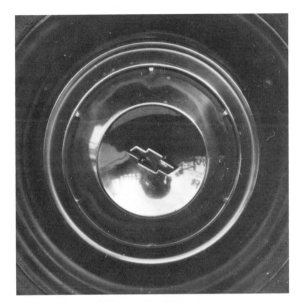

1968 standard Hub Cap.

1967-68 optional Wire Wheel Cover.

1968-70 optional Full Wheel Cover

1967-68 optional SS Full Wheel Cover

WHEELS & WHEELCOVERS

1969 standard hub cap (can also be used with trim ring).

1968-69 14" Rally wheel with trim ring and hub cap.

1969 Z28 15 x 7 Rally wheel, trim ring, and cap.

1968-70 optional "5-spoke" Full Wheel Cover

1969 optional "6-spoke" Full Wheel Cover

WHEELS & WHEELCOVERS

1970 optional Full Wheel Cover.

1970-75 optional 14 x 7 Rally wheel, trim ring, and cap.

1970 Z28 15 x 7 wheel, trim ring, and cap; continues standard through 1981.

1971-75 optional Wire Wheel Cover.

1971-73 optional Full Wheel Cover.

1973 optional Full Wheel Cover; available through 1980.

313

1973-74 14 x 6 Rally wheel, trim ring and cap.

Rally wheels also look well without the customary trim ring.

1975-77 optional Rally wheels in 14 x 6 or 14 x 7.

1976-81 optional Custom Styled urethane/ steel wheels; 14 x 7

1979 optional aluminum Turbine Wheels.

1978-81 color-keyed Rally wheels, with bright trim ring and hub cap.

1980-81 optional Aluminum Wheels; 15 x 7 on Z28; 15 x 6 on other models.

1981-81 Berlinetta wire wheel cover.

PRODUCTION STATISTICS

	1967	1968	1969	1970	1971	1972	1973
Total Units produced	220,906	235,147	243,085	124,901	114,643	68,651[+]	96,752[+]
Convertibles	25,141	20,440	17,573	n/a	n/a	n/a	n/a
Z28	602	7,199	**19,014**	8,733	4,863	2,575	11,575
Typical Options As A Percent of Total							
SIX cylinder	26.6	21.7	15.0	10.1	9.8	7.0	3.7
V8 engines:							
standard	73.4	78.3	85.0	45.1	49.0	40.3	38.5
upgraded				44.8	57.8	52.7	57.8
Automatic transmission	56.2	56.4	57.6	73.1	79.4	82.7	82.1
4-speed	21.5	20.2	23.9	15.0	9.3	8.5	11.8
AM radio	78.8	82.0	84.6	88.7	83.6	79.1	64.2
AM/FM Stereo or Tape	2.8	3.1	3.6	6.9	11.6	15.2	26.2
Air Conditioning	12.8	15.3	18.1	30.9	37.1	46.2	51.2
Tilt Steering wheel	3.6	2.3	3.0	5.4	7.3	5.4	13.6
Power Steering	41.7	49.0	57.3	74.2	81.3	87.2	std
Power Brakes	8.3	10.2	6.7	n/f	n/f	42.6	88.4
Power Windows	2.2	1.4	1.4	n/a	n/a	n/a	0.2
Vinyl Top Roof	23.7	32.8	41.1	34.6	33.4	34.8	32.4
Tinted glass:							
Windshield only	37.1	25.8	1.2	n/f	0.7	0.8	1.5
all	15.7	27.8	47.2	57.1	58.7	64.3	70.5
Dual Exhausts	16.3	21.7	26.4	17.0	12.9	13.3	25.6
Limited Slip Differential	14.4	15.6	21.0	15.8	10.3	11.1	19.4
Wheel Covers	67.9	62.9	46.2	61.5	49.9	n/f	26.8
Cruise Control	0.1	0.1	n/f	n/a	n/a	n/a	n/a
Styled Wheels	n/f	n/f	19.2	12.2	34.4	44.3	64.5
Clock	18.2	17.3	21.7	12.4	9.0	10.8	50.3
Power Door Locks	n/a	n/a	n/a	n/a	n/a	n/a	n/a
Rear Window Defogger	n/a	n/a	n/a	n/a	n/a	n/a	17.7
Remote-operated mirror	n/f	n/f	n/f	n/f	n/f	n/f	n/f

n/a option not available
n/f figures not reported
std Standard equipment

[+]a strike lasting almost six months
limited production and sales

	1974	1975	1976	1977	1978	1979	1980
Total Units produced	151,008	145,775	182,981	218,854	272,633	282,582	152,021
Convertibles	n/a	n/a	n/a	n/a	n/a	n/a	n/a
Z28	13,802	n/a	n/a	14,347	54,907	84,879	45,143
Typical Options As A Percent of Total							
SIX cylinder	14.7	20.5	20.8	14.3	13.6	7.8	n/f
V8 engines:							
standard	56.5	58.2	48.2	6.6	20.0	92.2	n/f
upgraded	28.8	21.7	31.0	79.1	66.3		
Automatic transmission	85.2	86.8	87.5	89.8	87.9	88.1	n/f
4-speed	7.4	6.0	6.2	6.2	9.7	10.5	n/f
AM radio	60.6	53.5	38.0	31.0	27.3	21.9	n/f
AM/FM Stereo or Tape	26.3	27.6	38.9	39.0	40.6	49.3	n/f
Air Conditioning	52.5	53.0	60.6	66.1	71.4	78.2	n/f
Tilt Steering wheel	15.7	21.6	25.5	35.4	42.9	51.6	n/f
Power Steering	std	std	std	std	std	std	std
Power Brakes	91.3	85.4	91.7	95.1	96.2	98.2	n/f
Power Windows	n/f	7.3	10.4	14.2	18.7	28.8	n/f
Vinyl Top Roof	25.2	18.4	13.6	9.0	4.3*	1.9**	n/f
Tinted glass:							
Windshield only	1.6	1.8	1.8	2.0	2.4	3.4	n/f
all	78.3	77.6	78.5	83.0	85.5	87.6	n/f
Dual Exhausts	22.7	n/f	n/f	n/f	n/f	n/f	n/f
Limited Slip Differential	17.4	6.1	7.0	8.0	12.0	13.7	n/f
Wheel Covers	22.8	20.3	14.6	10.0	5.4	3.7	n/f
Cruise Control	n/a	n/a	0.5	11.0	17.2	28.5	n/f
Styled Wheels	64.5	71.0	78.9	79.0	97.1	90.8	n/f
Clock	75.6	46.6	47.9	58.0	61.8	68.4	n/f
Power Door Locks	n/a	3.8	7.6	9.2	11.7	18.9	n/f
Rear Window Defogger	22.5	24.1	30.7	33.0	34.9	45.0	n/f
Remote-operated mirror	93.0	88.5	89.9	94.0	95.3	96.5	n/f

* Plus 3.6% Removable Glass Roof Panels
**Plus 11.9% Removable Glass Roof Panels

figures from Chevrolet Motor Division Production Records

CHEVROLET PROTECT-O-PLATE

The Protect-O-Plate is a metal identification card, specific to the vehicle, which contains much assembly data of interest to Owners. It was intended to allow Dealers to identify and define characteristics of a car when it was returned either for service or Warranty repairs. Thus, local Chevrolet Dealers are provided with the extensive coding necessary to decipher the plates, and are generally quite willing to advise Owners about details of their cars.

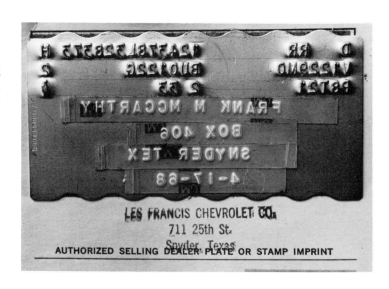

The following information can be ascertained from de-coding this 1968 Protect-O-Plate: (1) The car is a Camaro Sport Coupe with a V8 engine; (2) built in Los Angeles, the 228,373-th unit for the model year; (3) Matador Red Exterior; (4) Red Interior; (5) it's engine was built in Flint, on Dec. 29th, 1967, and is a true Z28 engine; (6) it's rear axle was built by Chevy Gear & Axle on Jan. 22nd; (7) The car was assembled in February '68 (8) it has a Holly carburetor; Power Disc Brakes and AM radio; (9) Transmission is Muncie 4-speed, built December 21.

Protect-O-Plates vary from year to year. From a reading of this 1969 version, it is determined that the car is (1) a Camaro Convertible with V8 engine; (2) built in the Norwood plant; (3) #126,908th unit (Camaro sequence numbers started at 500,000 that year); (4) carburetor built by Carter; (5) Tonowanda-built engine; (6) engine built March 27, 1969, a Type 50 for use with 4-speed; (7) Rear axle built by Chevy Gear & Axle on March 4th; and (8) vehicle assembled in April of 1969.

The Protect-O-Plate is normally affixed to the vehicle's warrenty and is delivered to the original Owner along with the Owner's Manaual and any additional necessary instruction materials.

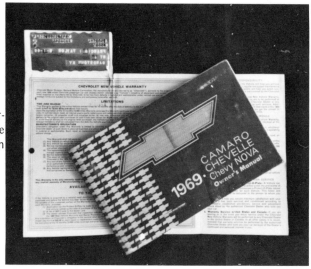

Fifteen years had passed since Camaro burst on the automotive scene and captured its share of the market. It had grown from a light, responsive, sporty car through an age of aggressive response into a twilight period as a luxurious dreadnaught; all the while persisting largely unchanged in a climate that saw an energy-conscious public turn away.

During this time, a total of over two-and-a-half million units were produced, indicating that there were those who understood its unique qualities. While often compared to that other advanced Chevrolet product line, the Corvette, in performance and response, it was perceived by an entirely different segment of the population. Never to receive the mildly anti-society aura of that car, it attained a strong following of its own among a more subdued element.

Changing perceptions as to size and quality entered into a necessary change in 1982, but remaining behind are the two-and-a-half-million cars that preceeded it. More durable than many, these vehicles are fairly abundant; many of the earliest are still driven daily. It is possible to restore virtually any of these cars; it is even more possible today to acquire examples that need little but refreshening. The forces that brought Camaro to the fore at the beginnning are still in effect; larger and larger numbers of people turn to this car as a collectible vehicle.

Camaro was an excellent-looking car when it was born; it performed well as a family car; it took the kids to the doctor, the family to the ballpark. Camaro raced on Sunday, and it was outstanding in professional competition. Camaro became an air-conditioned, power-assisted, stereo-equipped luxury liner, yet it did all of these things with quiet elegence. Camaro truly is

. . . Chevy's *Classy* Chassis

Readers seeking additional information on the subject may wish to consult the following:

For additional historical perspective —
"The Great Camaro"
Lamm-Morada Publishing Company
Box 7607
Stockton, California 95207

For contemporary association —
The Camaro Club of America
Box 5037
Kansas City, Missouri

The Pace Car Club
3335 Sackville Road
San Antonio, Texas 78247

For parts and information:
Chevy Parts Ltd.
570 El Cajon Boulevard
El Cajon, California 92020

Arizona Camaro Parts
4101 East Karen
Phoenix, Arizona 85032

Z & Z Automotive
233 No. Lemon
Orange, California 92666

Classic Camaro Parts
P.O. Box 4277
Palm Springs, California 92263

Specialized Investments of Houston
Box 36742
Houston, Texas